Conscience

CONSCIENCE

Writings from
Moral Theology
by Saint Alphonsus

Translated by
Raphael Gallagher, CSsR

Liguori

Imprimi Potest:
Stephen T. Rehrauer, CSsR, Provincial
Denver Province, the Redemptorists

Published by Liguori Publications, Liguori, Missouri 63057
To order, visit Liguori.org or call 800-325-9521

ISBN 978-0-7648-2814-0

**Cataloging-in-Publication Data
is on file with the Library of Congress**

Liguori Publications, a nonprofit corporation, is an apostolate of the Redemptorists. To learn more about the Redemptorists, visit Redemptorists.com.

Printed in the United States of America
23 22 21 20 19 / 5 4 3 2 1
First Edition

Contents

Acknowledgments

When I began this project twenty years ago, a number of people were very supportive, and I am happy to acknowledge them here. Fr. J. Robert Fenili, CSsR, was patient in correcting my Latin errors. Dr. Francesco Bonomo worked with me as the initial idea was to have a bilingual translation into English and Italian. I hope he will be encouraged by the semi-completion of this initial idea and complete the Italian translation. Avvocato Riccardo Dalla Vedova was a mine of information on Italian jurisprudence. Being himself a Neapolitan, he had an innate sense of the factors that shaped Alphonsus de Liguori.

As a text began to emerge, I had the benefit of many insightful comments from Patrick Hannon, professor emeritus of St. Patrick's College, Maynooth, Ireland. My confreres, Fr. Con Casey, CSsR, and Fr. Terence Kennedy, CSsR, studied my text and offered me many wise suggestions.

My Provincial in the Dublin Province, Fr. Dan Baragry, CSsR, generously facilitated my retirement arrangements to give me the time and space I needed to complete this work. I lived in various Redemptorist communities since my retirement: Rome, Paris, Dublin, and Limerick. I benefited from the friendship of confreres, especially Fr. Brendan Callanan, CSsR, and Fr. Brendan McConvery, CSsR. They helped me realize there is more to life than worrying about probability.

The bridge to a publisher was provided by Fr. John Kingsbury, CSsR, coordinator of the North American Conference of the Redemptorists, who agreed to bring my translation to the attention of the Spirituality Commission of the Conference. I am very grateful to the North American Conference for funding the project. When Liguori Publications agreed to publish this work, Máire Ní Chearbhaill provided professional help in preparing the manuscript for their consideration.

The president and publisher of Liguori Publications, Fr. Byron Miller, CSsR, helped me throughout. The same professional attention was afforded to me by the staff with whom I had contact, especially Mary Wuertz von Holt, director of sales, marketing, and product development; Chuck Healy, sales and customer service manager; and Tom Heine, developmental editor.

Fr. Michael Brehl, CSsR, the Superior General of the Redemptorists, has been a continuing personal support to me. His love for and loyalty to our founder strengthened my conviction that making St. Alphonsus better known was worthwhile.

Introduction

I TAUGHT MORAL THEOLOGY FOR NEARLY FORTY YEARS. References to St. Alphonsus de Liguori were frequent, for the most part repeating what others wrote. The realization that I had not paid attention to his most distinctive text on moral theology began to bother me. For the past twenty years, occasionally during semester breaks when I was a teacher and more consistently since my retirement, I have studied that text.

His original *Treatise on Conscience* is the opening tract of his monumental *Theologia Moralis*, written in Latin. As I grew in appreciation of the original text, I developed an aspiration to share its approach with a generation who find Latin difficult to understand. The translation aims at accuracy rather than literary flourish. There are differing views about the theological merit of Alphonsus. The rationale of my translation progressively developed a limited focus: present what Alphonsus himself said, leaving what others say about him to another day.

Every translator is a traitor: *traductor traditor*. I have avoided a verbatim translation, preferring what flows better in English to a rigid transliteration. On occasion, I have changed verb tenses, transposed subjects and objects, divided sentences, and added a word here and there to make the reasoning clearer. The original uses ecclesiastical Latin. I am mindful that today's reader is not likely to be accustomed to the grammatical constructions of this genre. Some important words, such as *opinio* and *sententia*, allow for differing English translations. I have let the context of their use give me flexibility. There is a further problem with the Latin style. Some of the articles are dry and didactic, and they remain so in my translation. Other articles are more like narratives, stories, or cases. I have tried to remain faithful to that technique when Alphonsus uses it. For understanding the treatise, the most important articles are the legal arguments of the text and the theological interpretations of Thomas Aquinas in the corollaries. Words matter, both in the Latin original and in the English translation. Words that are suitable in the juridical language of the text are not always the words that are appropriate in the theological controversies of the corollaries. Nonetheless, I have tried to be as consistent as possible in the linguistic style.

Alphonsus wrote the treatise for students. The translation maintains this didactic focus. The textbook style is deliberate. The translation is based on what I consider the best available critical edition, that of Leonard Gaudé (1905). An updated critical edition is needed. Meanwhile, I am confident that the edition used here is of a sufficient scientific standard to merit presentation in an English translation. The other Latin edition that has been widely used is Michael Heilig's (1852). I believe it is of a lesser quality than the edition by Gaudé.

When I first gave serious attention to the translation of the text, I focused on being a trustworthy translator. My preoccupations were Latin grammar and syntax, the choice of the more felicitous phrasing, and a desire not to betray the thought of Alphonsus. I did not start with the idea of a commentary, envisaging an occasional footnote instead. This would have been simpler for me, but I would have run the risk of offering an eighteenth-century text to a twenty-first century audience in too bald a form. The commentary eventually reached a point where it had become longer than the text, which would be disproportionate. The slimmer commentary printed here aims to give a scaffolding for the text, inviting the reader to enter the world of Alphonsus and offering indications for application today.

The novelty of this book is that it presents, for the first time, an English translation of a classic text of moral theology. I am not competing with the commendable historical-theological studies of L. Vereecke, S. Majorano, M. Vidal, L. Gaudé, D. Capone, or A. Amarante. I have benefited much from their research, incorporating some of it into my commentary. Alphonsus labored on this text over a thirty-year period. It is the part of the moral theology that is most noticeably stamped with his own style and convictions. I have the simple desire to present, in English, the Latin text of Alphonsus on conscience that is, beyond doubt, his most notable contribution to moral theology.

The confidence that the moral theology of Alphonsus is structured on a distinctive methodology matured as I worked on the text and commentary. Its historical significance is generally acknowledged. Can we learn from it now? The tedious work involved in the translation and commentary is my personal answer. Alphonsus presents, in the treatise on conscience, a distinctive way of understanding the moral judgment of conscience. Understandably, this is within the ecclesiology of his time. The demands of moral judgment are different in the Church that is emerging after the Second Vatican Council. Pope Francis is often mentioned for a remark he made in an interview (July 2013) about a young gay man who was a good person and doing his best: The Pope said, "Who am I to judge?" Nevertheless, someone has to judge, and the only one who can do this is the conscientious person. The treatise of Alphonsus retains an actuality in its insistence that the starting point of moral reflection is a consideration of how conscience decides.

Alphonsus intended this treatise as an introduction to moral theology. What conscience means for us, and what moral theology involves as a contemporary science, have changed appreciably. The commentary acknowledges these changes, suggesting analogous applications here and there.

While working mainly with the critical edition of Gaudé and consulting various editions of the moral theology printed during the lifetime of Alphonsus, I also took advantage of internet resources. I encourage readers of this text to do the same.

I made some editorial decisions for the exposition of this text. I present the first three chapters (up to Article 63) as a continuous text. There is a commentary on each of the articles. I present the two corollaries separately and offer no direct commentary on individual articles. I use the corollaries as the most substantial material for the commentary on Chapter Three of the text. The corollaries merit a separate commentary, article by article. My choice has been dictated by the scope of this book. The textual differences in the editions of Heilig and Gaudé are notable at this point, evident principally in the numbering of the articles. They take diverse approaches to the understanding of the sixth and later editions of Alphonsus, based on their understanding of the separate text of Alphonsus *(De usu moderato opinionis probabilis)* and the better way to incorporate it into the presentation of their own editions. The differences are more material than substantial.

This book, therefore, is not a critical edition of a classic text. I leave that exacting task to others. However, endnotes are offered for the contemporary reader to have an idea of the type of texts cited by Alphonsus. Here, too, I have made a personal editorial decision about how to do this. Alphonsus inserts his quotations into the body of the text itself. His manner of citing authors is inconsistent. Gaudé puts them in order in a series of footnotes, and adds some of his own where he was able to clarify what text

Alphonsus was referring to. In ordering my notes, I have followed the text of Alphonsus in the sixth edition of 1767 and compared it to the Gaudé edition of 1905 and the Heilig edition of 1852. I have standardized the methodology of the endnotes to fit the scope of this book, which is to present the text of Alphonsus as clearly as possible in English.

My purpose in the notes is simple: give the names of the authors, their dates, and the title of the main book cited in that note. I have not tried to establish the date of first publication or the edition cited by Alphonsus. A critical edition would evidently demand a very different approach. My references to the authors cited are to the principal work referred to at that location; other details are minimal. Notes should help a reader, and my presumption is that the readers of this volume will be primarily interested in what Alphonsus himself has to say. If my notes stimulate interest in further study, that would be a bonus.

Regarding detail in the endnotes, I have made an important exception, giving the precise textual references for Thomas Aquinas. These were the critical texts for Alphonsus. They are easily accessible today, unlike many of the obscure contemporary authors he cites.

The short bibliography of primary and secondary works refers only to works that I actually consulted. The internet has been an invaluable asset to me, but it can be unreliable as a primary source when dealing with a historical text.

Note on the Preface to *Theologia Moralis*

Alphonsus published the first edition of his moral theology in 1748. This was, in effect, a commentary on another work by a German Jesuit, Herman Busenbaum (1609-1668). In the subsequent eight editions, Alphonsus added a preface explaining his understanding of moral theology to which the tract on conscience was the entry point. He urged his readers to begin by reading the general preface in order to appreciate the sense of the complete work. It remains good advice.

Alphonsus accepts the legal nature of moral theology as it was understood after the Council of Trent (1545-1563). Law was the undisputed matrix.

In placing conscience as the entry point, Alphonsus is within the tradition of Catholic theology that was evolving since the thirteenth century. Law was considered to be the optimal guarantor of freedom. He was strongly aware of the fact that law-centered theology could degenerate into legalism. On the other hand, he did not accept the separation of law and freedom that was emerging in the Reformation churches. The dignity of conscience was, for Alphonsus, a personal one within an acceptance of the Church as guarantor of the interpretation of the law of God.

When Alphonsus says he is seeking a middle way between extremes, this is to be understood constructively. He was not looking for a compromise that reduced tensions to the lowest common denominator. In moral decisions for Catholics, salvation is at stake.

The conception of moral theology as a law-based discipline is one aspect of the ministry of the Church at the time Alphonsus was writing. The careful way Alphonsus outlines the steps in reaching a moral decision within a system of principles guarantees the dignity of a personal conscience. The claim of law to its rights is relatively straightforward. The claim of conscience to its rights is more challenging. Equity in the application of the law is the lodestar to protect conscience from an overbearing legalism.

Historical Background to the *Treatise on Conscience*

The gestation of the *Treatise on Conscience* translated in this book is a complicated story in itself. I refer interested readers to the works of Amarante, Vidal, Gaudé, Capone, and Majorano for the details of a fascinating publishing odyssey. Here I am simply giving minimal information for someone reading the text for the first time:

1696   Birth of Alphonsus de Liguori in Naples

1732   Foundation of the Redemptorist Congregation

1748   *Theologia Moralis*, first edition

1753-1755   *Theologia Moralis*, second edition, which includes the preface that is translated in this book

1765   Publication of *Dell'uso moderato dell'opinione probabile*. After the publication of the first edition of *Theologia Moralis*, Alphonsus was involved in public debates explaining and defending his system of moral theology. This 1765 work is the most significant of his publications on the matter.

1767   *Theologia Moralis,* sixth edition. The *Dell'uso moderato dell'opinione probabile* publication of 1765 is included in Chapter Three of the *Treatise on Conscience.*

1787   Death of Alphonsus de Liguori

1871   Alphonsus de Liguori is declared a doctor of the Church by Pope Pius IX.

1905   Leonard Gaudé publishes the four-volume critical edition of the *Theologia Moralis,* in which the *Treatise on Conscience* translated in this book is the opening tract.

1950   Alphonsus de Liguori is declared Patron of Confessors and of Moral Theologians by Pope Pius XII.

PART ONE

Treatise on Conscience
by Alphonsus de Liguori

PREFACE OF ALPHONSUS DE LIGUORI
TO *THEOLOGIA MORALIS*

To be read to enhance understanding of the whole work

The specific aim of our tiny Congregation of the Most Holy Redeemer is to be free to give missions. With the necessary work of the missionaries comes the duty of directing consciences by instructions and confessions. Therefore, for a number of years, I had been thinking of preparing a treatise on moral matters for the young students of our fraternity. I wanted one that would navigate a middle way between views that were too rigid or too lax. I finished the work, but it was much too hastily given to the printers. Others were pleased, but I was dissatisfied. Many things were either not well expressed or were explained in a muddled way. When I thought about giving the matter a more thorough analysis, as well as using a clearer method, I turned my mind to preparing a second edition. I have sought to redact everything in a better order and to give more thoroughly the most useful doctrines from other books. I also reformulated a number of opinions which, with the passage of time, I was able to go over more carefully. I am not embarrassed by this, just as St. Augustine was not ashamed to retract many opinions. In fact, St. Thomas did so too, as Cajetan, Catharinus, and Capreolus testify. Indeed, the angelic doctor himself admits: *although I wrote otherwise in another place.* Even Cicero said that *to change is good advice for the wise* and in another place: *it is never praiseworthy to persist in the one view.*

It will not appear excessive that I undertook this work as something that I needed to do since I have studied so many works dealing with moral science. Indeed, when I had read a lot of authors, I found some who were more indulgent to those who said (as Isaiah says in chapter 60, verse 30) *not for us those things that are right, speak to us those things that are pleasing.* They put little cushions under peoples' heads and let them settle down to a miserable life of sin. Undoubtedly, it does a lot of damage to the Church of God to be hearing from followers of these authors, since the greater part of people of a lax way of life agree with them. On the other hand, I found some who did not know how to get accustomed to condemning a certain type of extreme rigorism. They confuse counsels with precepts, and burden consciences with new commands. They do not spare a thought for human weakness, nor do they remember some advice from the sacred canons: *in those matters on which the law has not expressly stated something, you are to proceed with equity, always being inclined to the more human position. Accordingly, you will see what can be demanded of people, considering motivations, times, and situations.* In this way, those people make the yoke of Christ intolerable, when it should be light. They exclude many people from the path of salvation, as St. Ambrose said: *there are among us those who have the fear of God, but not in an informed way, laying down more harsh precepts that the human condition cannot sustain.* Both extremes are very dangerous. The first opens up, through laxity, the wide road to perdition. The second, as the very learned Cabassutius says, threatens souls with ruin in a double way—an erroneous conscience and desperation. Many, having heard this rigid doctrine, slip into mortal sin or, thinking that there is mortal sin when there is not, are terrified with the enormous difficulty of it all. Imagining that it is not possible for them to be saved in that way, they interiorly abandon caring about their salvation.

It is for this reason that I have been thinking about publishing a new work that steers a medium path among opinions that are too severe. I wished for a book that would neither be so extensive that it would be difficult to read, nor so brief that it would be deficient in many aspects. You will find here all those questions and moral matters which are more useful in practice. I sought views that were in greater conformity with the truth in each particular question, which took quite a lot of labor on my part. For a number of years, I consulted as many books as possible from the classic authors, those of rigid as well as of benign views, using, as far as I could judge, the most recent editions. I was especially eager to annotate the doctrines of St. Thomas, which I have sought to look at in their sources. Besides, for the more complex controversies, I have consulted the more recent theologians.

You will find here, in addition, canonical and civil texts that are pertinent, annotated in their appropriate place through diligent study. Likewise, you will find the propositions that have been condemned and (a most useful thing) the up-to-date decrees of the supreme pontiffs, especially the bulls and decrees recently published by our Holy Father, Pope Benedict XIV. I have, as well, expanded on many things that I have learned from the apostolate of missions and confessions rather than from books. In order to keep a solid method, I decided to use the *Medulla* of Herman Busenbaum. It is not that I approve of all the opinions of this author; it is only that I follow his method rather than that of other authors because it seemed to me very well suited to explaining moral matters. Thus, in accordance with my principal aim, I wished to be of more benefit to the young recruits of our Congregation. I took care to note down matters in the appendices in a way that could be more easily grasped. In all of this, I was concerned that I would succeed more in clarity of argument rather than elegance of language.

In the choice of opinions, my main concern was always to prefer reasoning before authority. Before I offered my own judgment, I tried to be completely indifferent with regard to every question, lest I made a mistake, and I rid myself of every tinge of passion. That is sufficient for you, kind reader, to know that I did not hesitate in this latest edition to change quite a few views that I had expressed in earlier editions. Moreover, I took care to expound my view of most questions in terms of their greater, equal, or lesser probability. I did this taking my own limitation into account, lest I leave the reader in doubt like those authors who give so much space to the views of others that they do not bother to offer their own views to the readers. Where I did not find a convincing argument for one side, I was not prepared to condemn the opposite one, unlike others who far too easily disapprove of opinions which many and serious authors hold. Some of these opinions you will find in the finely written works of our Holy Father, Pope Benedict XIV, whom I praised above, which are replete with all types of learning. He records these opinions but not without judging them, and he often relies on them. (May we be well distant from those who carelessly give little attention to this point.) He even uses these views quite a lot, and he instructs the Christian faithful relying on them on many occasions, as can be seen in his bulls.

Gentle reader, I wish to remind you not to judge that I necessarily approve of opinions simply because I do not condemn them. Anytime I faithfully explain them, with their reasoning and those who support them, I do so that others may come to a judgment, using their prudence as is their duty. Finally, you are to note that when I call some opinion more true, it is not that I hold the opposite opinion to be probable, even if I do not expressly condemn it as improbable. In addition, when I call one of the opinions more probable, with no judgment being given about the other opinion being probable, I use the phrase *non audeo damnare* (I do not venture to give a judgment) not because I understood it to be probable but the matter is left to the judgment of more prudent people.

MEMO OF ALPHONSUS DE LIGUORI
TO THE *TREATISE ON CONSCIENCE*

Take note, dear reader, that I have burned both ends of the candle in giving meticulous consideration to the opening *Treatise on Conscience*. It is the one that begins the path toward all moral theology. It was my wish to provide a more accessible study-outline for my students. Notice how, in the personal commentary I have added [material] taken from a treatise other than my own is clearly marked differently. I decided, also, to insert the interpretations of another author respecting his own divisions of the treatise. Most people would consider this to be the best method, since it allows for the necessary distinctions and links.

CHAPTER ONE ARTICLES

CHAPTER ONE

The Meaning of Conscience

Different Aspects and the Order to be Followed

ARTICLE 1
The remote and proximate rule for human actions

There are two rules for measuring human actions. One is more distant; the other is more immediate. The *distant* or material way of determining is from divine law. However, the *immediate* or formally correct way is through conscience. Even though conscience ought to conform to the divine law in everything, the goodness or evil of human actions becomes known exactly in the way that conscience understands it. This is what St. Thomas teaches: "Human reason is the rule for the human will by which its goodness is measured."[1] He is clearer in another work: "A human action is judged virtuous or wrong according to the good as properly understood: the will is directed to this, by itself, and not in accordance with the material object of the act."[2]

We will firstly consider the proximate rule which is *conscience*, and then the remote one which obviously concerns *laws*.

ARTICLE 2
Conscience and synderesis

Conscience can be defined: it is the judgment or practical instruction of reason by which we judge what is to be done here and now because it is good or avoided because it is evil.

Conscience is called a practical directive, to distinguish it from *synderesis,* which is the speculative knowledge of the universal principles of the good life, such as: "God ought to be worshiped. What you do not wish for yourself, you should not do to another." You will find this in St. Thomas.[3]

ARTICLE 3
Different types of conscience

Conscience can be categorized as *upright, erroneous, confused, scrupulous, indecisive,* and *probable.*

The *upright* conscience commands what is true. Therefore, a person who acts against a conscience in this sense commits a sin. The apostle states[4] that "anything that does not come from faith" (namely, from the instruction of conscience), is a sin, as Estius[5] and others explain.

Pope Innocent III supports this view: "Whatever is done against conscience builds the road to hell."[6]

A conscience is definitely *erroneous* when it prescribes something false as if it were true. Moreover, this type of conscience can be either vincible or invincible. It is vincible when the person acting could or should have corrected the error. This can be the case either because one already notices the error, or at least has a doubt about it. The person is aware of the obligation to overcome the error but still neglects to eliminate it. Saint Antoninus,[7]

Navarrus,[8] Suarez,[9] and others like Silvius and Cajetan give this as the standard teaching from St. Thomas.[10]

However, the Salmanticenses[11] and Castropalaus[12] along with Azor,[13] Suarez,[14] Vasquez,[15] Bonacina,[16] and Wigandt,[17] point out that, in the case of invincible ignorance, it is not required to take extraordinary care to overcome an error. Common ordinary care is enough. In the strict sense, ignorance is invincible when it is morally impossible to overcome it. No thought or doubt about the error enters the person's mind when acting, not even in a muddled way. This applies both while the person performs the action or determines a motive for doing it. The treatise *On Sins* in Book 5 will explain this more fully when we deal with the level of awareness needed to call something a sin.

ARTICLE 4
Following a vincibly erroneous conscience

Therefore, we assert that a person with a *vincibly* erroneous conscience *always* sins, whether acting in accordance with or against such a conscience. The person sins by acting against it, because one chooses an evil that is judged to be evil. There is evidently sin in acting in accordance with such a conscience, because a person who could and should overcome the error does not remove it and irresponsibly performs the act.

ARTICLE 5
Following an invincibly erroneous conscience

Secondly, we affirm that a person with an *invincibly* erroneous conscience not only does not sin by acting in accordance with it.

Indeed he is obliged to follow it in all circumstances. Here is the reasoning for both points. A person does not sin because, though the action in itself may not be good, nevertheless it is good according to the conscience of the person who acts. A person is bound to follow such a conscience (which is the proximate measuring standard) anytime it recommends the person to act in this way.

ARTICLE 6
Gaining merit

Not merely does the person who acts with an invincibly erroneous conscience not sin, but *more probably even gains merit,* as Fr. Fulgentius Cuniliati[18] and others correctly think. Here is the reasoning. In order to call some action good, or at least not imperfect, it is sufficient that the action be guided by the directive of reason and prudence. Therefore, in acting, provided the person does so prudently, one undoubtedly ought to be rewarded in view of the good purpose for which the action is performed. This good purpose could be the glory of God or charity for the neighbor and the like. In the same way, a person who does something good but comprehends the action to be evil is deprived of merit because of the immoral purpose intended.

ARTICLE 7
Answering some objections

Franzoja[19] objects that a bad action can never be a source of merit, and he quotes St. Thomas as support:

Good is caused by the integrity of factors, evil [is produced] by any single defect. Hence, for anything that the will seeks, it is enough for it to be either actually bad by its nature or to be understood as bad. To call it good, it must be good in both senses.[20]

Regarding this view, it should be answered that the angelic doctor is speaking here about good understood absolutely and unconditionally, and not about good understood relatively or contingently. Such is precisely the case when conscience, as the proximate rule of action, is not culpable about how it understands something. That is what the angelic doctor teaches, as already indicated: "A human act is judged virtuous or immoral in the way the good has been apprehended, insofar as that is what the will is of itself directed to, and not according to the material object of the act."[21]

Fr. Concina[22] is now closer to our view, although he had argued earlier that actions based on an erroneous conscience (even an invincibly ignorant one) could not be capable of either goodness or merit. He writes:

It could happen that a person, while performing an action that is materially bad, also performs a number of good actions, undoubtedly with the intention of pleasing God.... We say that these actions are good and meritorious, although the act performed may be materially bad, it is not to be qualified as a guilty act....The materially bad action, not being a voluntary one, is not a reason to ascribe evil to those actions.[23]

Saint Bernard endorses this more convincingly. He teaches that a subject who, with a good intention, obeys a superior, acts with merit even though at the material level the action is unlawful. This is how he expresses it:

> I would say that a person is praiseworthy on the sole basis of a religiously motivated intention. Clearly, a person will not be deprived of a just reward for an action that is some way not good, provided the will is good.[24]

ARTICLE 8
Invincible ignorance regarding the precepts of natural law

There is an initial question: *Can a conscience be invincibly ignorant regarding precepts of the natural law?* The answer will be brief. This can happen in the case of intermediary conclusions and of those that are at some remove from first principles. It cannot happen in the case of immediate and proximate conclusions (from the first principles). Examples would be the case of taking an owner's property against their will, killing an innocent person, and suchlike. This is the commonly accepted opinion, as we will prove later, using first and foremost the authority of St. Thomas. We will do this in the second treatise, *On Laws,* number 170.

ARTICLE 9
Desire, actions, and sin

There is a second question: *Can conscience be considered invincibly erroneous in a person who desires to accomplish evil*—take fornication as an example—*judging incorrectly that the simple desire of fornicating is not a mortal sin if, in fact, fornication does not occur?*

Sanchez[25] and Granado[26] propose this as the more probable view, asserting that the person sins only materially. Their reasoning is: although the person chooses a bad object, he still invincibly believes that the desire in itself does not inflict an injury on God. However, I would never hold this opinion to be probable. I could never believe such an opinion is sound. It would propose that a person who deliberately wishes to perform an action that he knows offends God could believe without guilt that God was not offended. Such a person effectively desires to carry out something which he certainly knows will turn him away from God.

You may say, however: How can a person sin formally by his desire if he is ignorant of its malice? Here is my answer: although it can be granted that the person is ignorant about the wrongness of the internal act, he surely recognizes the evil of the external act. If, therefore, a person wishes to carry out an act, already recognized as evil, in what way can he be excused from sin? Everyone can discern through the light of reason that they are bound to obey their Creator. Therefore, when a person deliberately wishes to do something that he knows God forbids him, at the same time he has to realize that he is acting wrongly. Although reflexively there is no sin, because he thinks that only the external act is a sin, in practice the person is already sinning. He desires to negate the obedience due to God at the time he is contemplating the sin to be completed.

You might continue to maintain that many rural people do not acknowledge this in the case of immoral desires. They believe that it is only sin when the external act is completed. My answer is that such people are quite deceived in believing that they are not bound to confess as sins something not completed in action. Accordingly, the prudent confessor ought to judge that when a person consents to complete a sin, he truly and formally sins. He is turning away from God with a defective will. In view of all these considerations I, along with other more recent experts, consider the opposite opinion to be not sufficiently probable.

ARTICLE 10
The perplexed conscience

We proceed to outline another type of conscience. A conscience is *perplexed* when a person is caught in the middle between two precepts. He believes he sins no matter which one he chooses. Take, for example, the case of someone who perjures himself in court to protect the life of a plaintiff. On the one hand, he is uneasy because the precept of religious respect for God forbids perjury. On the other hand, led by error, he is guided by the law of charity for a neighbor. He does not know what to do. How to proceed in this type of situation can be answered in the following way. If a person can postpone the action, he is bound to defer it while he gets the advice of well-informed people. If, in fact, he cannot postpone the decision, he is bound to choose the lesser evil, preferring not to break the natural law over not contravening human or positive divine law. If, however, the person cannot determine which might be the lesser evil, no matter which choice is made, a person does not sin. The reason is that, in such situations, the freedom necessary for formal sin is missing.

ARTICLE 11
The scrupulous conscience

Finally, we deal with the *scrupulous* conscience. It is necessary to treat this at greater length. A scrupulous conscience is one that, for a silly motive and without a reasonable basis, a person frequently lives in dread of sinning when there is in fact no sin. (A scruple is a mindless grasp of something.)

There are signs of a scrupulous conscience: (a) *Stubbornness in making a judgment.* The scrupulous person rejects the advice of wiser people, consults all over the place but accepts the judgment of no one. Indeed, the more views he listens to, the more muddled he becomes. (b) *Frequent changes of judgment* for frivolous reasons. As a result, there is indecisiveness in acting as well as mental disorientation, especially with regard to external actions such as the celebration of Mass, the recitation of the breviary, or the administration and understanding of the sacraments. (c) *Having incongruous ideas* about the many circumstances that were, or could have been, present in some action. (d) *Dread of sin in everything,* and mentally holding out against wise guidance and even against one's own judgment. Consequently, the scrupulous person is never content with the guidance of one confessor, and often seeks out another one regarding the same act. They wonder whether it is possible in conscience to be free from guilt by following the advice given.

ARTICLE 12
The remedies for scruples

Here are the therapies to be applied to scruples of this type. Once the confessor recognizes from the above signs that the penitent is scrupulous, he should give these directions: (a) He should strongly nurture the virtue of humility. In fact, scruples often have their root in the vice of pride. (b) The penitent should be warned against *reading books that give rise to scruples,* as well as avoiding conversations with scrupulous people. (c) He should not delay excessively in examining his conscience, especially about whatever is bothering him the most. (d) He should avoid *idleness,* where the mind is often filled with ridiculous notions. (e) The penitent should immediately commend himself to God to obtain the support to comply with the directions of his director. This is the most important point of all. In fact, the only remedy that can be applied to illnesses of this type is to submit completely to the judgment of one's superior or confessor, as all the fathers, theologians, and spiritual masters agree.

Hence, it will be of enormous benefit in calming consciences bothered by scruples if the confessor brings to their attention the exceptionally wise authorities that I list. Natalis Alexander writes: "So that scruples can be spurned, the scrupulous person should act against them, supported by prudence and under the judgment of a holy and learned director....If someone has a finicky and credulous conscience, it is legitimate for that person to follow the advice of his pastor."[27]

Saint Antoninus, following Gerson,[28] confirms this:

A person who categorically refuses to trust the advice of superiors and of prudent people in order to get rid of such scruples, and acts against their advice, makes several mistakes. Many people are deceived in this because of naiveté, not knowing how to distinguish between the things that the higher part of the soul assents to, and those that the lower part of the soul permits without the approval of the superior part.[29]

Saint Bernard agrees. He said to one of his scrupulous devotees: "Go away, and with trusting me you can celebrate." Someone once said: "Would that St. Bernard were my superior! Candidly, what I see is the mediocre wisdom of my superior and I would not dare hand over my conscience to such a person."

Saint Antoninus answers, once more relying on Gerson:

Whoever says and understands things in this way is out of their mind and is wrong. You are not handing yourself and your salvation to a human merely because he is prudent and well educated, even devout, but because he is your superior....For this reason, you are not giving obedience to a human but to God. Be especially careful so that, while looking for security, you do not fall into the treacherous gutter of poor judgment and presumption.[30]

On this point, St. Philip Neri used to say to his penitents: "Those who desire to make progress in the way of God submit themselves to a learned confessor whom they obey as if he were God. Whoever acts in this way has security by having a justification for all their actions."[31]

He used to speak of having trust in your confessor because God would not permit the confessor to make mistakes. There is no more secure way than complying with the will of your director when you act. There is nothing more dangerous than self-direction in coming to a personal judgment.

Similarly, St. Francis de Sales, explaining how to be a spiritual director, writes on the basis of Blessed John of Ávila: "There is no better way of being certain that we are open to the will of God than by humble obedience to the instructions of a director."[32] The Glossa confirm this: "If there is truly a doubt about a precept, one is excused from sin by virtue of the goodness of obedience, even if in fact the precept was a bad one."[33] A similar thing is said in the chapter *Quid culpatur*, casus 23, q. 1.

Saint Bernard remarks: "Whatever a human, acting in the place of God, instructs is not to be taken as if it could displease God; instead, it is to be completely accepted as if God himself ordered it."[34] Saint Ignatius of Loyola states: "Obey in everything where sin is not discerned (that is, as in the Declaration), in those matters in which there is clearly no sin."[35] Blessed Humbert adds: "Unless what the superior orders is plainly evil, it is to be accepted as if it had been ordered by God."[36] Blessed Denis the Carthusian comments: "In doubts...whether something is against a command of God, rely on the order of the superior because, even if it is against God, nevertheless, on account of the goodness of obedience the subject does not sin."[37] Saint Bonaventure repeats the same teaching.[38]

ARTICLE 13
The importance of obedience

For these reasons, the confessor should be firm with people tormented by scruples. He should persuade them that a person is totally secure when he accepts the advice of the confessor by submitting in everything where there is not evident sin. He is not simply obeying a human being, but God himself who says: *whoever hears you, hears me; whoever rejects you, rejects me* (Luke 10:16). The confessor will impress on the penitent, who refuses to obey the instructions of the confessor, that he is putting his salvation at a great risk. Such a person exposes himself to losing not only peace of heart, piety, and progress in virtue but, in fact, risks losing his mind and bodily health. (How many scrupulous people, who do not accept the necessity of obedience, go crazy!) What is worse, they risk the loss of their souls. Indeed, the scrupulous person can reach such a state of desperation that they think of taking their own lives. This happens to many, or else they become so despairing about their own salvation that they lose any sense of restraint and engage in all sorts of vice.

ARTICLE 14
Use of general rules

Furthermore, with this type of penitent, the discerning confessor should be content to offer broad general rules rather than detailed ones. With scrupulous people, precise rules almost never sort out what they are to do. The reason is that they always doubt whether the proposed precept could be valid for the case in question. This often seems to them to be different from a case previously solved by the confessor. Concina is correct about this: "Once penitents have been given the general rules of direction, they should not be running back and forth to their director, pestering him with utterly irksome questions...they should banish all their scruples and fantasies with the general rules they have been given."[39]

ARTICLE 15
Various fears of scrupulous people

Broadly speaking, scrupulous people are tormented in three different ways. Some are tormented by bad thoughts to which they frequently believe they have assented. Others have doubts whether past confessions were sufficiently complete. There are others who have a fear of sinning in anything they do.

With regard to penitents who fear they have assented to any bad thought (for example: against faith, chastity, charity), the confessor should insist that the penitent should totally reject giving in to these scruples, insisting that it is not the bad thoughts that are sinful but only those deliberately consented to. On this matter, the confessor should never omit to apply the rule wisely handed down by the doctors of theology; judge those who have an extremely delicate conscience as not having sinned unless they know with moral certainty that they have consented to a grave sin. Fr. Alvarez[40] says it is impossible for sin to enter the soul of someone who abhors it without the person being clearly conscious of the sin. It is often helpful that the confessor insist, with scrupulous people, that they stop confessing sins of thought of this type, unless they are absolutely certain that they have consented to these thoughts and are ready to swear to this.

ARTICLE 16
Anxiety about confessions

Some scrupulous penitents are constantly tormented about past confessions and fear that the confessions were either materially incomplete or lacking in proper sorrow. If the person has already made a number of general confessions or has been careful over a long period to confess frequently, the confessor is to be resolute on the following point. He is to insist that they are no longer to think of past faults, they are not even to mention them in confession unless they can swear that they have certainly committed mortal sin and, besides, that they have never before confessed this sin. This is what is taught by Azor,[41] Bonacina,[42] Becanus,[43] Coninck,[44] Laymann,[45] and others. They say that it could occasionally happen that a person is so tormented with scruples that, even if it is clear that something has not been confessed, the penitent is not required to confess it at this point. Wigandt confirms this with a pertinent comment:

The penitent who consults over and over again about sins that have been already confessed is not to be given a hearing....though it is possible that some sins may not have been confessed, nonetheless, on account of the serious damage to himself and the grave danger of being perpetually trapped in such anxiety, he is entirely excused from the [obligation] of integrity in confession.[46]

In this case, the confessor is to robustly insist that the penitent obey him. If he refuses to obey, he is to be deprived of Communion and, as far as possible, be dealt with in a fairly blunt way. With scrupulous people who are obedient, treat them with gentleness. With those who are lacking in obedience, the maximum rigor and strictness is to be shown. Deprived of the stable anchor of obedience, such people can never be cured.

ARTICLE 17
Those who fear sin in every action

Finally, there are scrupulous people who fear sin in every action. The confessor is to insist that they despise their scruples and work against them where no evident sin is apparent, so that they act in a free manner. Quite regularly, the fear of sin, where there is no sin, is to be attributed to one's reasoning being affected by excessive fear. The value of imposing this rule is that they can overcome the scruples and so avoid being driven out of their minds or end up being completely incapable of acting at all. Afterward, they are to refrain from accusing themselves of such actions in confession. It is possible that by doing this, they are sometimes in error. However, they do not sin by reason of the obedience which they ought to show to their confessor.

This is the sensible teaching of Sanchez,[47] as well as St. Antoninus,[48] Gerson,[49] Valentia,[50] Corduba,[51] as well as the Salmanticenses,[52] Cajetan,[53] Navarrus,[54] Castropalaus,[55] Bonacina,[56] and Filliuccius.[57] They say that the scrupulous person is always under a grave obligation to oppose the scruples. This is because the anxiety caused by scruples carries a risk of severe damage to their spiritual progress or their mental and physical health.

ARTICLE 18
When there is actual fear

It does not matter whether a person acts with a scrupulous conscience or if they *actually fear* they are sinning. According to the general and correct opinion taught by Concina,[58] Roncaglia,[59] Anacletus,[60] St. Anthony, the Salmanticenses,[61] as well as Navarrus, Cajetan, Bonacina, and many others, the scrupulous person who acts in this way sins minimally. The reason is that a scrupulous conscience, or a dictate of conscience that has its origins in scruples, cannot nullify the previous assent the person gave to act in the exact way advised by the confessor. To put it another way, as Fr. Concina says: "Doubt cancels assent. It is clearly otherwise with a scruple which is to be distinguished from a doubt. Scruples therefore can be seen as those little clouds which can somehow obscure the judgment of the intellect, without entirely suffocating it."[62]

This holds especially if obedience to the confessor promotes actions against scruples in situations where guilt cannot be clearly determined. This can be deduced from the chapter titled *Inquisitioni 44, de sent. Excom.* where the Pope [Benedict XIV] declares it to be safe to follow the advice of the pastor in rejecting scruples. These are the words: "It can be lawful to act according to your pastor's advice (if your conscience is fickle or fearful because of nerviness or credulity)." This does not contradict another text taken from the chapter *Per tuas 35, de simonia* where the Pope lays down that anyone who has an overly scrupulous conscience should not proceed to higher orders unless their conscience has first been sorted out. The response here is that it is not merely a scruple that is being discussed, but more properly an error about who should be ordained, as the Glossa explain: "This would constitute an erroneous conscience. It is explained as such in the text: unless he gets rid of the error."

ARTICLE 19
The basis of a proper judgment of conscience

We finish on a practical note. The scrupulous person acts freely if he always bears in mind the virtue of obedience by which he may undeniably put aside the fear caused by scruples. It is not required that he make this decision in each particular case. It is enough that he discard his scruples on the basis of the command given him by the confessor. It is sufficient that he acts with a judgment that has been previously made to go against his scruples. On the basis of past experience, with this sort of conscience, such a judgment exists already in the conscience, either virtually or habitually, even though it is clouded over by shadows. This is even more the case with a scrupulous person. He acts in a state of such confusion that he emphatically does not have a formed and properly discerned conscience, such as that required to constitute sin, as John Gerson correctly writes:

Conscience...is formed when...after deliberation and discernment, it is determined and settled by a definitive judgment of reason that something is to be done...or avoided. To do something against such a formed conscience...is a sin. Indeed, fear or a scruple of conscience occurs when... the mind fluctuates between doubts, neither knowing what is for the best, nor knowing what he is more obliged to do. However, he does not wish to omit anything which he knows would be against the divine will. Acting against a conscience full of fear or scrupulosity is not always a sin, even though it could be quite dangerous (that is: unless the fear is erased as being foolish, especially if that agrees with the counsel of one's director).[63]

Gerson adds: "As far as possible [fear] is to be banished and extinguished." He also writes:

Scrupulous people should act decisively against their scruples, and they should do this in a sure-footed way. There is no better way to conquer and overcome them than by hating them, and usually this is not possible without the help of another's advice, particularly that of a superior. Otherwise, unwarranted fear causes us to fall or it leads to silly presumptions.[64]

For scrupulous people, Natalis Alexander says we should follow the rule given by Blessed Albert the Great and St. Antoninus: "Everything else being equal, when it comes to a choice between a severe or benign judgment, the benign interpretation is to be preferred."

There is more to be said about the doubtful and probable conscience. We will treat these separately.

CHAPTER 2 ARTICLES

20. *What is an indecisive conscience?*

21. *Speculative and practical doubt*

22. *Acting with a conscience that is practically doubtful*

23. *Qualms about the type of sin*

24. *Solving practical doubts*

25. *Speculative doubts*

26. *Reflex principles*

27. *Doubt: promulgation and abrogation of law*

28. *Doubt and vows*

29. *Vows and probability*

30. *Fulfilling a vow carelessly*

31. *Obligations toward superiors*

32. *Doubts about various issues*

33. *Doubt about the validity of a marriage*

34. *Doubts about paying outstanding debts*

35. *Doubts about ownership*

36. *Different evaluations about the rights of ownership*

37. *Obligations of owners when there is a doubt*

38. *Doubts about receiving Communion*

39. *A further doubt*

CHAPTER TWO

The Indecisive Conscience

ARTICLE 20
What is an indecisive conscience?

A conscience is hesitant when it cannot come to a judgment between alternatives. As a result, it remains ambivalent and indecisive. There are two types of indecisive conscience. One is practically hesitant about which action to take; the other is speculatively unsure regarding the truth of the action. Indecision may also be classified as negative or positive. A doubt is called *negative* when neither side presents probable reasons, but only weak ones. A doubt is considered *positive* when both sides (or, at least, one side) offers a serious motive. This requires that it proposes a sufficient basis to form a probable conscience, even though some anxiety about the opposite view remains. Therefore, positive doubt almost always coincides with the probable opinion. This will be the topic of Chapter Three.

ARTICLE 21
Speculative and practical doubt

Hence, a doubt may be either speculative or practical. The doubt is *speculative* when it is about the truth of a matter; for example, whether a war is just or unjust, whether painting on a feast day is forbidden or permissible, whether baptism using distilled water is valid or null, and so on. A *practical* doubt concerns the moral uprightness of the action; for example, whether I may take up arms in a particular just war, whether I can paint on this particular feast day, whether I may baptize this child with distilled water. Thus, one must always distinguish between what is *true* and what is *permissible*. A speculative doubt can, at least indirectly, touch on what is permitted. For the most part, however, a speculative doubt concerns what is true, while a practical doubt is concerned about what is permissible.

ARTICLE 22
Acting with a conscience that is practically doubtful

Having considered all of this, our first assertion is that it is never licit to act with a practically doubtful conscience. If a person acts in this way, he sins, and the sin is of the same species and gravity as the doubt. This is because those who leave themselves open to the danger of sinning, sin in doing so, in accordance with the Book of Ecclesiasticus 3:27: "Whoever loves danger will die in the danger." Therefore, if a person doubts whether an action is a mortal sin, it is a mortal sin if it is chosen.

ARTICLE 23
Qualms about the type of sin

What about a person who knows that something is evil but is un-clear whether it is a mortal or venial sin? Can the person act with such a doubt? Some hold that the person sins gravely or lightly in precisely the way the object of the sin is grave or light in its spe-cies. This is the view of Vasquez,[65] Sanchez,[66] and others. There are some, however, including Azor,[67] Bonacina,[68] and Castropalaus,[69] who think that such a person always sins gravely. Others, along with Navarrus,[70] Valentia,[71] Granado,[72] and many more, hold it is sufficiently probable that the person only sins venially. If a person is only slightly aware, and does not advert, even in a confused way, to the danger of grave sin or to the need for weighing up the case, the object chosen is surely not per se a grave sin. I would add a comment: even if the person has a delicate conscience.

ARTICLE 24
Solving practical doubts

The person with a practical doubt about what to do must at least get rid of the doubt. This is ensured by determining the goodness of an action through the application of a principle that is certain or by employing a reflex principle. We will explain this in the *Dis-sertation on the use of the probable opinion*. This is the only way a person is capable of forming a conscience with practical certain-ty, thus making it possible for him to act. For people incapable of doing this (think about a poorly instructed person), they are obliged to consult their parish priest, or confessor or some holy and learned person; then, they act according to the advice given.

A person who is genuinely in doubt but who comes to realize that, everything having been properly considered, the doubt is groundless, can then quite correctly put his qualms aside and without further reflection perform the action (as Continuator Tournely[73] correctly writes). In that case, since the malice of the act is unknown, the ignorance is completely involuntary, because the difficulty could not be resolved by studious scrutiny. This is the teaching of the angelic doctor.

ARTICLE 25
Speculative doubts

Our second assertion is that it is licit to act with a speculatively doubtful conscience, provided the person proceeds on the basis of other reasons or reflex principles. In so doing, the person judges in practice that the action is certainly morally upright. According to the scholarly argument of Bishop Abelly, these are the probability or improbability of an opinion. An example would be whether this war is probably just or doubtfully so. There are different methods by which we judge the *uprightness* of an action, for example, whether it is licit for a subject to take up arms in this particular war ordered by a prince. This is in line with St. Augustine's teaching as will be explained later.[74] How it is possible, using reflex principles, for a conscience to be properly morally formed regarding the integrity of an action will be clarified in the *Dissertation on the probable opinion*, which we will give in the corollaries at the end of this treatise.

ARTICLE 26
Reflex principles

The most important of these principles is: *a doubtful law cannot impose an obligation that is certain.* The truth of this principle, which is not denied even by those who uphold the most rigid opinion, will be more clearly established in the dissertation mentioned above. *Consider what will be said there.*

From this first principle, a second is derived: *Possession is the better condition.* Indeed, when a doubtful law obliges a person in only a marginal sense, he is at any rate not obligated and is therefore free from the obligation of the law. In such a case, because the law is doubtful, one is at liberty to use the freedom that the person definitely possesses. Saint Thomas says so: "What is not prohibited by the law is considered licit."[75] Indeed, this is the second principle, although there are some who try to devalue it by saying that it applies only in a courtroom or, at most, in matters of justice. I do not understand, however, why it cannot be applied to every situation.

The only question that can be brought up about a moral doubt is whether it is the law or liberty that is in possession. Those opposing probabilism say that the law is always in possession. We hold, quite justifiably, that sometimes it is the law that is in possession, and at other times it is freedom. This is surely correct when the law has not yet been promulgated. I believe this is the appropriate question. No one can deny the principle: possession always creates a presumption [of ownership]. Therefore, in a case where the law is in possession, the law is to be defended; in a situation where freedom is in possession, freedom is to be protected.

In determining, therefore, which side has possession in circumstances that are doubtful, we must establish which side has the presumption. The presumption correctly stands with the side that is not bound to prove possession. It is the opposing side which has the obligation to provide proof: *a fact is not to be presumed unless it is proven*; this is another principle approved by *leg. 2, de probation*. In doubt, therefore, a fact is not to be presumed. It has to be proven. If a fact is certain, for instance, that a marriage has definitely been entered into, but there is a doubt whether it was celebrated in a proper ritual way, then a different principle ought to be used: *in doubt, whatever was done should be presumed to have been correctly done.* Said in other ways: *in a doubt, what was done is presumed to have been done according to the law* or *the value of an action is to be endorsed.*

ARTICLE 27
Doubt: promulgation and abrogation of law

From what has been said, we can deduce that *if a law has been imprecisely formulated or dubiously promulgated,* it does not oblige. It cannot oblige for the reason that possession remains on the side of freedom. Likewise, we hold that *if there is a doubt whether the law has been understood to have been promulgated,* we are not bound to fulfill it. The reason is: insofar as some part of the law is dubious, then the law is not in possession. On the other hand, however, *if a law has been clearly formulated and definitely promulgated,* but a doubt later arises whether it has been abrogated, revoked, or dispensed from, it must be obeyed because it remains in possession. *Even if there is a doubt whether a law that is per se just has been established,* it should be followed, because there is a presumption regarding its reception based on another principle: *in doubt, the fact is to be presumed that we are obliged to do what has been established by law.*

ARTICLE 28
Doubt and vows

The second implication is that what has been said about a law applies to a vow, since a vow is similar to a specific law that the person imposes on himself.

Therefore, if a person doubts whether they have taken a vow, they are not bound to fulfill it. This is the common understanding taught by Cabassutius,[76] Suarez,[77] Sanchez,[78] Anacletus,[79] and the Salmanticenses,[80] along with innumerable others. Likewise, *if a person doubts whether something has or has not been included in a vow*, the person is not bound by the part about which there is doubt because it is not in possession. This can be deduced from *Ex parte 18, de censibus*. When a person has taken some kind of vow and later begins to doubt whether they are obliged to the greater or lesser part of what was promised, they are only bound to the lesser part. Similarly, the Glossa notes: *in doubts, whatever is most agreeable may be followed.*

On the other hand, if a person is certain that a vow was made but hesitates whether it was fulfilled, the person is bound by the vow because in this case the vow is in possession.

ARTICLE 29
Vows and probability

Several authors raise another question: If someone has only a probable reason to judge that the vow has already been fulfilled, is he nonetheless bound to fulfill it? Many reply in the negative, namely Roncaglia,[81] the Salmanticenses,[82] along with Leander, de Lugo,[83] and others. The stated reason is that, since the obligation of the law in that case is doubtful, the law's possession is likewise in doubt. In the past, I considered this opinion probable, guided more by extrinsic probability than by intrinsic probability. Now, however, after giving the matter more thought, I consider this opinion to have minimal probability. I now hold that the opposite opinion should be followed, in agreement with Concina,[84] Antoine,[85] Filliuccius,[86] Leander,[87] and others.

My reasoning is that if the doubt were about the taking of the vow, it is correct to say that there is no longer a duty to fulfill it, because freedom is in possession. But since the vow is certain, the freedom in question is still restricted by the obligation of the vow as long as the vow has not yet been certainly accomplished. The first view can be upheld only if there is enough probability to lead to *some level of moral certainty* that the vow has been carried out. What we have said about a vow is also to be applied to the case of satisfaction in *the sacrament of penance.*

ARTICLE 30
Fulfilling a vow carelessly

What about the case of a person who has taken a vow and then performs what was vowed without thinking of the obligation of the vow when doing so? It is very probable that he is not bound to fulfill the vow again, as Suarez,[88] Laymann,[89] Sanchez,[90] and Bonacina[91] teach, along with Azor,[92] Lessius, and many others. This position rests on the certainty that if the person had thought of the vow when acting, he would have wanted to fulfill the vow. The normal presumption is that anyone who has a general desire to fulfill obligatory duties would do so without having to perform an additional supererogatory action.

ARTICLE 31
Obligations toward superiors

A third inference can be noted. A *subject,* even though he is not obliged to obey a superior ordering something that is certainly illicit, *is still obliged to perform an action that is deemed doubtful, whether it is licit or not.* The reason is that a doubt does not cancel the authority of a superior who has the right to give the command. This is commonly held by Cajetan,[93] Continuator Tournely,[94] and many others, along with St. Antoninus,[95] St. Bonaventure,[96] Cabassutius, Soto, and others.

However, Soto, Continuator Tournely,[97] Lessius,[98] Sanchez,[99] the Salmanticenses, and others put a restriction on this view. It does not apply when what is commanded is seriously difficult or burdensome. This would be the case if, by obeying, the subject leaves himself or someone else open to the danger of significant spiritual or temporal damage. We will explain this more fully later when we are treating the particular precepts in *Book 4, Chapter 1, n. 47.*

ARTICLE 32
Doubts about various issues

A fourth conclusion can be drawn. A young person who is unsure whether he has completed his twenty-first year is not obliged to fast. What about a person who doubts whether he has reached his sixtieth year (on the completion of which a person is probably no longer bound by the laws on fasting, as we will explain in *Book III, n. 1026*)? Such a person is obliged to fast, because the precept on fasting is then in possession. The same is to be said regarding those who have a query about having reached *the age required for sacred orders* or for assuming a benefice: possession remains in favor of the precept.

The same is to be said when someone doubts whether midnight has passed and Saturday has begun: the person may not eat meat because the rule of abstinence on Friday remains in possession. The opposite is true if one has a doubt whether the day is actually *Thursday*: the reasoning is that, when due effort to come to a decision has been used, a person may legitimately eat meat, since at this point freedom is in possession. This is the view of Laymann,[100] Sanchez,[101] Busenbaum,[102] and many others.

ARTICLE 33
Doubt about the validity of a marriage

There is a fifth implication. After a *marriage* has been contracted in good faith, a doubt arises about its validity and *has not yet been properly analyzed*. The spouse with the doubt may not request the marriage debt but is obliged to render it. This is because the spouse who has no doubt retains the right to request it. *After a proper examination*, the person with the doubt may also request it. This is the more probable opinion supported by Soto,[103] Habert,[104] Wigandt,[105] Roncaglia,[106] Sanchez,[107] and the Salmanticenses.[108] (Please see what we will say in *Book VI, n. 903 and 904*.)

ARTICLE 34
Doubts about paying outstanding debts

Sixth, it can be inferred that when one is certain that a debt is owed, but is not sure if it has been repaid, a person is obliged to repay it. This is the shared teaching of Suarez, Vasquez, de Lugo, and others, along with Sanchez.[109] In the case where even the creditor has doubts about his rights, it is the opinion of Laymann,[110] Diana,[111] Sporer,[112] as well as Tamburini, that the debtor is bound only to repay in proportion to the amount in doubt. However, Laymann adds that he would not venture to condemn the creditor for demanding a full repayment.

ARTICLE 35
Doubts about ownership

At this point we put a question: *A person is in good faith about ownership, but has a hesitation about some portion of it. Is the person bound to repay it in proportion to his doubt?* If the doubt is equal between the *pro* and *contra*, the general opinion, as articulated by Sanchez with few dissenting voices, is that the owner is bound to nothing, based on *Rule 65 in 6º*: *In a case of parity of opinion, the position of the owner is stronger.* We know this from *Rule 128 and following* concerning various rules of law: *In a case of parity, the owner ought to be granted the stronger position.* However, what if the arguments against the owner are stronger?

The first view is that, even if the owner has a probable reason in his favor, he is bound to restitution in proportion to a larger consideration that is to be calculated. Even though the position of the owner is stronger in the case of equal doubt, it is not so in the case of unequal doubt. This is the view of Sanchez, along with Coninck,[113] Valentia,[114] and Ledesma from the Salmanticenses.[115]

The second view, however, which is more commonly held and more probable, explains that the owner is not bound to any restitution, unless it is morally clear that the property belongs to another. This is the view of Castropalaus,[116] de Lugo,[117] Roncaglia, along with Laymann, Cardenas, Dicastillus, Tamburini, Diana,

Burghaber, and others among whom are Lacroix,[118] Mazzotta,[119] Sporer,[120] with Molina and St. Augustine who says: "An owner in good faith is properly so-called as long as he is unaware of claiming property that belongs to another."[121] This is true (according to Sporer) so long as there is a doubt about the other party's ownership and the current owner is unaware that what he possesses belongs to another. The principal reason for this view is that a person acquires a right through ownership in good faith.

The law defines possession as *the right of keeping something which one is not forbidden to have*. Therefore, the possessor maintains the right of retention while the doubt about ownership remains. This is true in the sense that, until a careful effort has been made to ascertain the truth, he can retain possession of the object. If after this thorough search has been made and the truth cannot be established, he can then use the object and even alienate it, with the proviso that the buyer is warned about the doubt raised about the item. In the face of this very convincing reasoning, Sanchez[122] changed the opinion that he supported previously and followed the second one. Also, Cardinal Sfondratus[123] says that one should not begin a court procedure against the person in possession unless one acts out of certainty.

From all of this, there seems to be little probability in what Roncaglia[124] says: if the reasons favoring the possessor are only slightly probable, he is bound to give the whole amount back, or at least most of it. Rather, if the arguments against the possessor are so probable that they form moral certitude against him, then the possessor is bound to total restitution. Otherwise, he is not required to make any restitution.

ARTICLE 36
Different evaluations about the rights of ownership

There is a second question: *What if there is a probable reason against the person in possession and none in his favor?*

The first view holds that if the probable argument favors the opinion that the item belongs to someone else, while the current owner has no support to say that the article is his, then it must be returned. This is not the case if there is some probability that the item might be his. This is the position held by Sanchez who cites Vasquez, Castropalaus, Renzi,[125] Tamburini,[126] and Viva.[127] He says that since the one in possession is faced with a probable opinion against him and none in his favor, there is moral certitude that the thing belongs to another.

A second view, held by Salas,[128] says that up to the point where the reasons against the owner produce some agreement, even though still not compelling, there is no morally certain agreement. It is simply a matter of opinion that includes anxiety [about the contrasting view] present in all opinions. Therefore, the holder can keep the item since possession prevails over all reasons that are not convincing.

The above opinions can be reconciled. It is certain that legitimate possession, which includes a right of retention, remains well founded as long as it is not clear that the object rightly belongs to someone else. This is generally taught by Castropalaus, Laymann, Sporer, and the others mentioned above with Lacroix.[129] Even Viva concedes this: "Good-faith possession is clearly a right that is certain. It ought to prevail against the rights of others that may be juridically probable but not morally certain."[130] The reason is that legitimate possession in itself creates a clear presumption for the justice of the possessor's [ownership], as Wigandt[131] and de Lugo[132] say. Therefore, even if there is a probable opinion against the owner and none in his favor, there still remains the presumption created by the fact of possession. This confers on him a right so solid that nothing else can overcome it, except a contrary judgment in law that is certain because of definite...reasons.

On this basis, the first view states that the person in possession is bound to make restitution when he is faced with a conflicting alleged agreement and has none in his own favor. This can be reasonably understood to mean that when possession is in some way weak, to the point that it becomes doubtful or may have been obtained in poor faith, then no legitimate presumption in favor of the possessor can be seen to arise from it. At this point, there is no probability that can come to his assistance; all that remains is the supposed judgment that what he possesses is the property of another. It would be different were he to have certain and legitimate possession in good faith. Then, possession alone, even if no other reasons were given to support it, would confer on him a right that is certain. This right could not be overturned except by opposing reasons that are certain, but not by a probable opinion that necessarily includes an element of fear [of the opposite opinion].

De Lugo clearly implies this when he says that possession itself has a usual presumption in favor of the person in possession. This remains unless he is deprived of it by the item being shown to belong to someone else through a proof that overrides the presumption given by possession. Hence, Lacroix[133] correctly concludes that, even if there may not be a probable argument in favor of the owner, as long as the petitioner has no argument except a probable one, the owner legitimately remains in possession. Possession confers a right of retention that is certain. Only certainty can prevail against it.

The same can be said of a marriage that is probably null: confer *Book VI, n. 904.*

ARTICLE 37
Obligations of owners when there is a doubt

There is a third question: *What about an owner in good faith who irresponsibly neglects to give due attention to resolve a doubt when it arises, but afterward the true owner can no longer be established?*

Lacroix,[134] Roncaglia,[135] and the Salmanticenses[136]—along with Sanchez, Lessius, and some others—say the owner is bound to make restitution for the part associated with the doubt. On the other hand, Castropalaus,[137] Bonacina,[138] and Tamburini—along with Diana and Ribellus—think that it is probable that, although he sinned seriously by not attending to the matter, by this stage, he is not bound to do anything. On the one hand, the damage done is doubtful and, on the other, the right of possession acquired in good faith allows him to keep the goods.

I think it is more correct to say that such a proprietor is bound to make some form of restitution (to the owner, or to the poor if the owner is unclear). The rationale is that the [present] proprietor culpably deprived the [previous] owner of the expectation he could have had of the goods. Because expectation has a value that can be estimated, then damage was surely done to the owner who clearly had such an anticipation. I think, however, that the restitution is not to be measured by the amount of the doubt. If the reasons on both sides were equal, the goods or their medium worth should be returned. [The restitution] should be less, and perhaps much less. This is because the expectation of the owner could not have been estimated at half the value of the goods, but at a much lesser value. There being equal probability of argument on one side, and the definite right of possession for the other [who now holds it], this latter right favors the owner and continues to do so. The possession of some actual thing has more value than possession of a hope.

1. Tamburini,[139] Villalobos,[140] and others note if the owner begins to have doubts on the basis of probable reasons, he is then bound to seek out the truth of the matter. This would not be the case were he to have doubts based on merely tenuous reasons.

2. Lacroix[141] notes along with Vasquez, Laymann, Castropalaus, Sanchez, Molina, and others, that when someone possessed something in good faith (including one who took on the ownership doubtfully) and then discovers that further investigation is impossible, is not bound to restore anything. Roncaglia[142] considers this view to be not improbable. The owner can legitimately hold on to any right involved.

ARTICLE 38
Doubts about receiving Communion

Another thing should be said. If there is doubt whether you have swallowed some food or drink, can you receive Communion? Sanchez, Roncaglia,[143] and the Salmanticenses,[144] along with others, answer that you cannot. They argue that the undeniable law of not receiving Communion without fasting is not satisfied by a doubtful fulfillment. They add that doing so would seem to imply grave disrespect.

Others, however, like de Lugo,[145] Castropalaus, Laymann,[146] Diana,[147] Lacroix,[148] Busenbaum,[149] and Sporer,[150] along with Sà, Cardenas, Medina, Gobat, and Bossio, affirm that with such a hesitancy you can quite correctly take Communion. Their reason is that the law about fasting is not a positive law that prescribes fasting as an absolute prerequisite for receiving Communion. Rather, it is a prohibitive law by which someone is restricted from approaching Communion when they have taken some food or drink, for fear that human food be mixed with heavenly food.

De Lugo[151] repeats the same view in accordance with the Second Council of Braga[152] that prohibited anyone who had eaten some food from consecrating an offering on the altar. The same is proposed by the Seventh Council of Toledo:[153] *no one can presume to celebrate Mass after having taken some food or drink, however small the amount.* A similar view is found in the Ecumenical Council of Constance:

> The praiseworthy authority of the sacred canons and the approved custom of the Church contained a value and still do. A sacrament of this kind ought not to be consecrated after taking a meal, nor is it to be received by the faithful without fasting, except in case of illness or other necessity conceded or admitted by law or by the Church.[154]

De Lugo[155] repeats this. I submit that the law of fasting is a prohibitive one, that is, against someone taking Communion after consuming food. Hence, it is necessary to prove that the fast was broken in order to forbid Communion. Therefore, in the case of doubt whether this is a situation in which the law applies, one is not bound to abstain from Communion since the person's freedom is still in possession.

De Lugo[156] makes the point that the law of the Church that a person should not take Communion after eating is not being disobeyed if the person, after proper examination, does not know if he has consumed something. A person can licitly take Communion if in doubt about breaking the fast. In this matter, Communion is only forbidden to someone who has (knowingly) broken the fast. The freedom to receive Communion is rightly in possession as long as the infringement of the fast is not clear. This way of reasoning does not seem to merit being disparaged as frivolous. At least in this case, the law prohibiting Communion does not seem certain and thus, as a doubtful law, it does not oblige, as will be explained in *no. 55ff.*

As to the other reason against [reception], that of irreverence, it should be answered that it is not considered a matter of irreverence when people exercise their right of freedom, especially if they approach Communion through a sense of devotion.

ARTICLE 39
A further doubt

The question can also arise whether *a person can take Communion if he has a doubt whether he has taken food or drink after midnight?*

De Lugo says no. Since a person knows they have eaten, but has a doubt whether they ate after midnight, it would seem that the burden of proof rests with them to show that they did not eat after midnight. Nevertheless, in line with many noteworthy persons, we say that if the reason adduced above (that the law is prohibitive, not positive) is valid for the first case, it is also for the second. The prohibition against receiving Communion is for those who have taken something after midnight. Therefore, if the fact that they have eaten must be proven so that they cannot receive Communion, so also must the fact that they ate after midnight be proven. Besides, this affirmative judgment is held also by other doctors named above, to whom can be added the erudite Fr. Eusebius Amort. He examines [the case of] one who has eaten when in doubt if the midnight hour had struck, and asks whether this person can take Communion the following day. He answers: "One can take Communion, because the position of the one in possession [of a right] is better, as long as there are no contrary presumptions so strong that even the person involved believes it more probable that the midnight hour has already struck."[157]

CHAPTER THREE, SECTION I ARTICLES

The Probable Conscience

ARTICLE 40
The probable conscience in broad outline

A conscience is probable when a person, supported by some probable opinion, forms for himself a reasonable practical command on the basis of clear reflex principles or on principles associated with them in order to act in a lawful manner.

At this point, it should be noted that there are various types of probability: the slightly probable opinion, the probable opinion, the more probable opinion, followed by the most probable opinion and, finally, the morally certain opinion. There is also the safe opinion as well as the safer opinion.

An opinion is *slightly probable* when it is based on some sort of foundation, but not one strong enough to deserve the approval of a prudent person. It is never lawful to use this type of opinion, as indicated by *Proposition 3*, condemned by Innocent XI, which states:

> Generally speaking, we always act prudently as long as what we do is based on some probability, either intrinsic or extrinsic, however slight, provided it remains within the bounds of probability.[158]

An opinion is *probable* when it is based on a solid foundation, either intrinsically from reasoning or extrinsically from authority. It is sufficiently probable for a prudent person to give assent to, even if there are qualms about the opposite opinion. An opinion is *more probable* when it is based on a more substantial foundation, even if there is a strong concern that the contrary opinion might also be considered probable.

A *most probable opinion* is one that is based on very serious grounds in a way that the opposite opinion would be considered questionable or doubtfully probable. It is always lawful to act in accordance with such an opinion. This is clear from *Proposition 3* condemned by Alexander VIII, which states: *it is not lawful to follow a probable opinion or even the most probable of the opinions offered.*[159]

A *morally certain* opinion is one that excludes all prudent fear of being mistaken so that the opposite opinion would be considered entirely improbable. Finally, an opinion is *safe* when it removes all danger of sinning. A *safer* opinion is one which removes even more definitely the danger of sinning, although it may not be based on more convincing reasons.

ARTICLE 41
Probability of fact and of law

Next, it should be noted that there is a difference between probability of *fact* and of *law*. *Probability of fact* is the probability concerning the truth of a matter or, if you prefer, the substance of something; for instance, whether a sacrament conferred with a particular material would be valid or null, whether a contract based on a specific type of agreement would be usury or not. *Probability of law* is concerned with the uprightness of an action, that is, whether it is lawful to confer a sacrament using a particular material, whether one should undertake a contract based on such an agreement.

ARTICLE 42
Probability of fact and liceity

Based on what has been said, we affirm that it is never lawful to use a probable opinion about a fact when there is danger of damage to another person or to oneself. The reason is that this kind of probability does nothing to reduce the danger of harm. If the opinion is false, damage to another or to oneself is not avoided. So, for example, if baptism conferred with saliva is in point of fact null, the infant remains unbaptized. Probability in favor of the opposite can do nothing to actually make it valid.

ARTICLE 43
The opinion to be followed in matters of faith

From this it can be implied that, in matters of faith and in all that concerns the means necessary for salvation, it is not lawful to follow an opinion that is either less probable (as foolishly presented in the *Proposition 4* condemned by Innocent XI) or even one that is more probable. We are bound to follow the safer opinion. Consequently, we are obliged to accept the safer religion, which is undoubtedly the Catholic one. Since every other religion is false, even if it appears to someone as more probable, embracing that religion and abandoning the safer one would mean there is no way to avoid the loss of eternal salvation.

ARTICLE 44
The opinion to be followed by a medical doctor

There is a second implication. A doctor is bound to use the safer remedy to benefit the patient. He may not use remedies whose benefit is less probable in place of one whose benefit is more probable or safer. As regards medical treatments, the more probable view is the one that is safer for the health of the patient.

ARTICLE 45
Can a less-safe medical practice be employed?

A doubt can be raised whether doctors can use a less-probable remedy in place of a more probable one, when there is not a certainly sure treatment. Azor, Aragon, Montesinus, Salas from among the Salmanticenses[160] answer in the affirmative. However, some of the Salmanticenses[161] themselves—with Soto, Suarez, and Bonacina—are in favor of the more probable view. Their reasoning is that doctors do not act only out of charity. They are also obliged in justice to look after the health of the patient in the best way possible, by reason of their profession and as implied in their contract with the patient who pays them.

ARTICLE 46
Distressing cases involving the seriously ill

A second doubt occurs. When hope has been given up about the health of a patient: Can the doctor apply remedies that he himself does not know are either helpful or prejudicial? There is a common opinion that, when there is no fixed remedy available but another one might probably help, the doctor may use it; in fact, he is obliged to try it. Confer the Salmanticenses.[162] It is also certain that doctors are not allowed to apply to the sick person, even one in a desperately ill state, a remedy which they do not know to be either beneficial or harmful, in order to experiment on the patient. This is commonly held by the Salmanticenses,[163] along with Navarrus, Azor, Castropalaus, Salas, Perez and others. The reasoning is that it is unlawful to perform an experiment involving the danger of the death of a sick person or of hastening the dying process. It is certain, moreover, according to Sanchez[164] and the Salmanticenses,[165] that if there is a remedy that is questionably helpful but certainly not harmful, it should indeed be given to the sick person.

With regard to the original question, however, there are two views. The *first view* is in the negative. The reason is (as given above) that it is never lawful to expose a sick person to the danger of death or to accelerate the dying process. This is the view of the Salmanticenses,[166] with Azor, Castropalaus, Silvestri, Villalobos, and others. However, the *second view*, which is sufficiently probable, and perhaps more probable, holds that it is lawful. This is held by Sanchez,[167] with Valentia, Busenbaum[168] likewise, also Bonacina, Filliuccius,[169] and Reginald Bardi among the Salmanticenses.[170] Their reasoning is: Since the case is critical, it is more in conformity with prudence and with the will of the patient (especially if the patient expressly consents to it) to apply the doubtful remedy that, were it omitted, would mean certain death. This view is considered certain by Antoine[171] when speaking about the profession of the doctor.

Sanchez moreover remarks, along with Navarrus, that even if the doctor cannot apply a remedy acting against his own opinion, it is lawful for him to administer it, if it is a cure approved by other doctors and the patient consents to it.

ARTICLE 47
The opinion to be followed by a judge

A third inference is that a judge is bound to adjudicate in line with the more probable opinion. He is obliged to do this by both divine and human law so that each party receives the rights to which they are due according to the weight of the evidence. This is the basis of the condemnation Innocent XI gave in *Proposition 2: I think it probable that a judge can give judgment according to an opinion that is even less probable.*[172]

Cardenas,[173] with others, correctly notes that if the accused is in legitimate possession of an item under dispute and has a probable reason to support him, a judge cannot deprive him of it even if the plaintiff can offer more probable reasons. Legitimate possession (as we explained in Art. 35) gives the person in possession a right that is certain. He can retain something until it is otherwise clear in law that it belongs to another. Confer my *Moral Theology, Book IV, no. 210, Qu. 2* where this is explained at length.

ARTICLE 48
Ministers of the sacraments

We can infer fourthly that, in conferring a sacrament, the minister cannot follow either a probable opinion or a more probable opinion about its validity. He is always obliged to follow the safe view, which is either the one that is safer or morally certain. This can be implied from *Proposition 1* condemned by Innocent XI:

> It is not unlawful to follow the probable opinion about the validity of a sacrament and ignore the safer view, unless this is forbidden by law, convention, or the danger of

incurring grave harm. For this reason, an opinion that is only probable should not be confined simply to administering baptism, priestly or episcopal ordination.[174]

ARTICLE 49
In cases of necessity

I said: *Unless it is a case of necessity*, because in extreme necessity it is proper to use any opinion, not only a probable one, but even one that is slightly probable, in favor of the sacrament. This is the view correctly proposed by Holzmann,[175] Antoine,[176] Cuniliati,[177] and others regarding the way in which a sacrament may be conferred conditionally. The reason is that the conditional conferral sufficiently makes up for any disrespect to the sacrament if, by chance, it were conferred invalidly. On the other hand, a proper necessity and a just cause are required for the conditional conferral of a sacrament. See what will be said in my *Moral Theology, Lib. VI, cap. I, de Bapt., no. 103: Et hic sedulo; et de Poenit., no. 482, in fine.*

ARTICLE 50
When the Church supplies jurisdiction

Many authors say that one can legitimately use a probable opinion where it is presumed that the Church will supply what is lacking. This could happen in the sacrament of matrimony to validate a contract that is only probably valid, if by chance the contract were null due to an impediment that the Church has the power to remove. In the sacrament of penance, likewise, jurisdiction is supplied for the confessor if he by chance lacks it. This view is judged to be the most common by Viva and Lacroix,[178] with Suarez, Lessius, Coninck, Reginaldus, and Sporer.[179] Dicastillus even calls it morally certain. De Lugo[180] together with Arriaga, Suarez, and Diana following Cardenas[181] claim this is the practice of the whole Church.

However, pay attention to Book VI of my *Moral Theology, no. 573* where many points are made about the manner and circumstances involved in presuming that a confessor's jurisdiction is supplied by the Church. As well, observe *idem, no. 572*, since the idea that the Church always supplies for jurisdiction in the sacrament of penance continues to be a common mistake.

ARTICLE 51
Receiving the sacraments

Next we can ask whether what we have said about administering sacraments applies also *to their reception, so that no one may receive a sacrament simply on the basis of a probable opinion?*

The first view supports this. It is held by Cardenas,[182] Viva,[183] and Lacroix.[184] Their reasoning is that the special reverence due to the sacraments demands that we do not leave them open to the danger of being ineffective. They say this on the basis of what was said in *Proposition 1*, condemned by Innocent XI, about the administration of sacraments. Reception of the sacraments is implicitly condemned because the same danger of deception about their effect applies also to their reception.

The second view rejects this. It is held by Pontius and Sanchez, along with Vasquez, Salon, Satyrus, Perez, and others following Cardenas. Sporer and Viva say something similar. It seems that they at least refrain from applying it to the opinions of those who make deductions in practice about receiving the sacraments. Their reasoning is that no one who uses a probable opinion is thinking about damaging the sacrament; nor do they believe the sacraments demand more respect than what is due to divine precepts. This view, as Master Hozes says following Cardenas, does not lose its probability due to the pope's condemnation. It is not clear that the proposition was proscribed on the basis of the reverence due to a sacrament or because of the charity due to the person receiving the sacrament. All these points notwithstanding, I do not think I should abandon the first view. The second view can hardly ever be verified in practice for people who are actually receiving a sacrament without a real danger to their soul.

ARTICLE 52
Dealing with doubts of fact

The fifth and final implication that we can draw is about the case of someone who has a doubt whether what he sees in the forest is a wild beast or a human. The person cannot kill it, even if it is probably or more probably a wild animal. If, in fact, the object is a human being, the probability or even the greater probability does not save the person from death.

Therefore, it can be said that, in all cases, it is never lawful to use a probable opinion in a doubt of fact whenever there is danger of harm or injury to a neighbor.

ARTICLE 53
Dealing with doubts of law

An opinion that is probable because of the probability of *law* is a different issue. In this case, anyone may use a probable opinion in forming his conscience in order to provide certainty for the uprightness of his action.

Now that we have explained the nature of opinion, we will describe our moral system.

CHAPTER THREE, SECTION II ARTICLES

The Moral System

On the Choice of Opinions That Can be Lawfully Followed

ARTICLE 54
Following a more probable opinion

Firstly, I say that when an opinion in favor of the law appears to be certainly more probable, we are absolutely bound to follow it. We cannot choose an opposite opinion in favor of freedom. The reason is that, in order to act lawfully, we ought to investigate the truth in undecided questions and follow it. On the other hand, when the truth cannot be clearly established, we are bound at least to follow the opinion that comes closest to the truth. This is the more probable opinion.

ARTICLE 55
The probable opinion

Secondly, I maintain that when an opinion in favor of freedom is merely probable, or is equally probable with an opinion in favor of the law, it cannot be followed simply on the basis of being a probable opinion. For an action to be lawful, probability alone is not sufficient. Moral certitude is required about the uprightness of the action, just as St. Paul tells the Romans (Romans 14:23) "For whatever is not from faith is sin" *(Omne autem quod non est ex fide, peccatum est)*. The text states "from faith" *(ex fide)*, that is, from a sure injunction of conscience. A person is persuaded in conscience that his action is right. This is how the phrase *ex fide* is explained by St. Chrysostom, St. Ambrose, and others along with St. Thomas.[185] Hence, I regard as false the claim commonly repeated by probabilists: "Whoever acts with probability acts prudently."

ARTICLE 56
When opinions are equally probable

Thirdly, I hold that in the case of two equally probable opinions making the same claim, any opinion that is less safe cannot be supported. As stated above, probability alone (note: *probability alone*) does not provide a guaranteed foundation for acting lawfully. Nevertheless, the opinion in favor of freedom, by having equal probability with its opposite in favor of the law, raises a serious doubt about the existence of the law prohibiting the action. As a result, this is sufficient at least for questioning whether the law has been adequately promulgated. In that case, since it is not promulgated, it cannot bind. This is all the more so for the reason that an uncertain law cannot impose a certain obligation. This is the view of St. Thomas that I follow myself and which appears undeniable to me. Then there is the authority of theologians, as we have seen, as well as of the Fathers (whose teachings will be seen in the First Corollary at *no. 66*; also confer Christian Lupus,[186] who compiled many authoritative statements of the Fathers). What is more, it is also certain for intrinsic reasons, which are not just ornamental additions but are certain and clear arguments, as will be proven.

ARTICLE 57
Law must be promulgated

The prince of theologians, St. Thomas, teaches the following: "Law is a kind of direction or measure for human activity through which a person is led to do something or is held back from it."[187] *The word comes from* ligando *because it is binding on how we should act.* From this, the holy doctor goes on to teach that this direction and measure must be clearly made known to people by promulgation. In this way, it may be applied to them and they can be held bound to observe it. He says:

> Law is laid on subjects to serve as a rule and measure. This means that it has to be brought to bear on them. Hence, to have binding force, which is an essential property of law, it has to be applied to the people it is meant to direct. This application comes about when their attention is drawn to it by the fact of promulgation. Hence, promulgation is required for a measure to possess the force of law.[188]

Law cannot oblige subjects unless it has been promulgated to them. This is an axiom everyone knows. "Laws are established when they are promulgated," writes Gratian.[189] The reason is evident. A law that remains in a legislator's mind is no more than a rough idea or intention of making a law; it does not have the real structure of a law that obliges subjects. This is why "law" is defined by St. Thomas as "an ordinance of reason for the common good which has been made by the authority who has the care of the community and which has been promulgated."[190]

There is no doubt [according to Franciscus Henno] that "promulgation is part of the essence of law."[191] As Ludovicus Habert correctly states, "Promulgation and the power of binding ...belong to the very purpose of law."[192] Cardinal Gotti adds that promulgation is a necessary prerequisite in order that subjects be bound by law:

> In order that a law oblige in practice, it is required, without exception, that it be made known to the subjects through promulgation.[193]

Dominic Soto expresses the same view: "No law has any power of law before its promulgation...it becomes established as law when it is promulgated."[194] He immediately adds: "There is, then, no exception to this conclusion." The French doctor Duvallius[195] writes in the same vein, saying that the eternal law could not have obliged people from all eternity because, as he puts it, *it is of the intrinsic meaning of genuine law that it be imposed on and promulgated to its subjects; and there were no subjects from all eternity.* Fr. Gonet repeats this: "The eternal law could not have obliged humans from all eternity because it was not promulgated."[196]

A similar idea is found in Lorichius: "[The eternal law] is promulgated to people when it was made known to them and continues to be known to them."[197] Even my bitter adversary, Fr.

Patutius, says: "All agree that promulgation is absolutely necessary so that law can have the power to oblige."[198] Someone may wonder why I brought together so many authorities to prove a teaching that no one really doubts. I want you to know that I have done this because the strength of my position is embedded in this very principle, namely, that a doubtful law does not oblige. We shall see this later.

At another point, St. Thomas, while holding this as a certain view, raises an objection to himself: "Natural law, which is law in the fullest sense of the word...needs no promulgation; therefore it is not of the essence of law that it be promulgated."[199] He answers his own objection: "The response to this is that natural law is promulgated by God so instilling it into people's minds that they can know it through their very being." To make this even clearer, Silvius adds:

In fact...then, the natural law is promulgated when a person accepts its knowledge as a dictate of conscience about what is to be done and what is to be avoided according to right natural reason.[200]

John Gerson teaches the same: "The law is a declaration made for the rational human creature, by which he knows what God judges about certain things which God wishes to oblige the human person to observe or omit."[201] Finally, Petrus de Lorca adds: "Just as promulgation is intrinsic and necessary for human laws, so the judgment of reason and understanding is intrinsic to the law of nature."[202] Because of this, without the judgment and knowledge of reason, there is no other way by which a law is sufficiently promulgated to impose an obligation on a person.

ARTICLE 58
Law must be promulgated as certain

For law to oblige, it must not only be promulgated, but it must be promulgated *as a law that is certain*. This point has to be firmly established: hence, I will be assessing it at length. There is a good reason, since it is necessary to repeat many things said elsewhere. Indeed, to be absolutely clear, it is from the strength of this foundation that our view derives its force, namely: an uncertain law cannot impose a certain obligation. We say, therefore, that no one is obliged to observe a particular law unless that law has been made clear to the person as certain.

My position is, as we saw, that it is necessary for law be promulgated in order for it to oblige. If a doubtful law is promulgated, what is promulgated is only a doubt, an opinion or a query as to whether there is a law prohibiting an action. What is promulgated is not a law. Hence, all accept that law, in order to be obligatory, must be certain, clearly made known, and certainly presented to and recognized by the person to whom it is promulgated. Let us pay attention to what is commonly said by theologians on this view or about this principle. Among all the teachers, St. Thomas best expounds it and offers proof. Saint Isidore states that, among the conditions for a law to be obligatory, it must be clear. This is certain also from canon law.[203] The same thing is also certain in civil law: *in doubt, no obligation is to be presumed.*

Saint Thomas, speaking about the eternal and natural law, teaches that in order for this to be our measuring rule, it must be most certain and made clearly known to us. Let us look at his own words and how he raises an objection to himself:

A measure should be most certain (take note of that). However, the Eternal Law is unknown to us. Hence it cannot be the measure which rules the goodness of the act of our will. [204]

He answers the objection in this way:

Although as dwelling in the divine mind the Eternal Law is unknown to us, nevertheless in some fashion it becomes known to us either through natural reason, which comes from the divine mind as its proper image, or through revelation given to us over and above the power of reason.[205]

The reason is clear why law ought to be certain. Since law, according to St. Thomas, is the measure and rule by which a person ought to take the measure and rule of his actions, it is impossible for these to be measured and ruled unless the measure and rule are certainly obligatory, and in a way that the person understands. The very learned Peter Collet writes:

For law to oblige, it is necessary that it be given as a rule, so that subsequently it can become known. Because law does not become known unless it is promulgated, this is the only way by which it can be indicated to us in a manner that demands obedience.[206]

The same view is given by John Gerson when he says that law, in order to be obligatory, must necessarily be made known to a person. Otherwise, God could not oblige the human person to serve him. Most noteworthy are the words of Gerson:

It is necessary that the ordinance and will of God be made manifest, since God, by his ordinance alone or only through his will, cannot impose obligation on a human being in an absolute way. In order to do this, it is necessary that God give equal notification of the one and of the other.[207]

Gonet is of the same view: "A person cannot be bound to conform to the divine will…except when the divine will is made manifest to us by a precept or a prohibition."[208] From this, he offers the argument that the sin of a human person depends on his willfully transgressing the law. If, in fact, he says, sin depends on the existence or nonexistence of the law, then sin would be a matter of luck or chance and not a matter of the will. This is a clearly absurd position. He writes:

Quite often it is a matter of chance, and not of the will, that a person sins or does not sin. It seems that what he does is in conformity or not with the natural law of which they are ignorant. This is indeed an absurd position, since the true and only cause of sin is the will which acts in a way that is not in conformity with the rules of morals.[209]

Silvius presents a similar view: "In reality, then…natural law is communicated to each one when one accepts the knowledge dictated by God on what, according to natural right reason, is to be done and what avoided."[210] Therefore, no one is bound by a law unless he knows, through right reason, that this law is necessarily to be followed. Fulgentius Cuniliati is of the same view, stating unequivocally: "Those to whom the law has not yet been made known are not violators…of the law."[211] Iodoch says the same. Lorichius has a comparable view: "The law is promulgated to people when it is made known to them, and it remains always known to them."[212]

ARTICLE 59
Human will and conformity to divine will

From all that has been said, the moral certainty of our view or, rather, the view of St. Thomas, is made abundantly clear. He explains it in many places, but most significantly when he offers this moral principle in a definitive way: "Nobody is bound by any principle except through the knowledge of that principle."[213]

All philosophers, with St. Thomas, explain the distinction between an opinion *[opinio]* and knowledge *[scientia]*. An *opinion* refers to the doubtful or probable comprehension of some truth. *Knowledge* in the true sense refers to the certain and obvious grasp of a truth. Let us listen to the sacred doctor himself. What St. Thomas understands under the term knowledge *[scientia]* is specifically a certain knowledge. This is obvious because he poses this question: "Does conscience bind?" He then responds:

> Thus...where the will is concerned, the relation between the command of a master and the imposition of the kind of obligation by which the will can be bound is like the relation between physical action and the binding of physical things through the necessity of constraint. However, the action of a physical agent never imposes necessity on another thing except by the contact of its action with the object on which it is acting. So, no one is bound by the command of a master unless the command reaches the one who is commanded; and it reaches that person through knowledge of it.... As in corporal things, an agent does not act on a body except through contact with it, so also in spiritual matters a precept does not bind except through knowledge.[214]

The image St. Thomas gives here could not be more clear and compelling to prove our view or principle, namely that an uncertain law cannot impose a certain obligation. The holy doctor says that knowledge of a precept is like a chain that binds the will. Wherefore, just as it is necessary that a rope be properly applied in order to tie up something, so it is necessary that a person have knowledge *[scientia]* of the precept so that his will is bound to do or to omit some action. Otherwise the person remains free. For this reason, as long as there is a doubt whether there is or is not a precept prohibiting or allowing something (as occurs when two opinions with the same weight of probability are competing with each other), then the person does not have knowledge *[scientia]* of the precept, and as a result the person is not bound to observe it. To further explain this, the angelic doctor adds in the same passage:

> But to see in what way (conscience) binds, it is necessary to know how the binding, metaphorically transferred from bodily realities to spiritual ones, brings with it the imposition of a necessity. The one who is bound must necessarily remain where he is bound, and is deprived of the capacity of going anywhere else.[215]

Just as, on the contrary, a person who is not really tied by some bond has the power of going wherever the person desires. Thus, whoever is not bound by knowledge of a precept is free from the obligation of the precept. For that reason, the holy doctor writes that law *[lex]* derives from binding *[ligando]*: *The word comes from* ligando ["binding"] *because it is binding on how we should act.*[216]

Saint Thomas confirms this view more strongly in another place where he asks: "whether it is necessary that an act of human will be conformed to the divine will in respect of what is good?"[217] He answers that it should, yet he raises the objection:

It seems that the human will ought not always be conformed to the divine will as regards the object it wills. But we cannot will what we do not know...yet what God wills for us we do not know in most cases. Hence our will cannot be conformed to the divine will as to the object willed.[218]

Thomas gives this answer:

Regarding the first point...we may know what God wills for us in some general way for we know that whatever God wills, he wills because it is truly good. And so, whoever wills a thing because of any aspect of goodness it contains, has a will conformed to the divine will with regard to the reason for willing it. Nevertheless we do not know what God wills in a particular situation, and in as far as this is the case we are not bound to conform our will to his.[219]

Thus, St. Thomas teaches that the human person, who always wills something according to its nature as good, is already in conformity with the divine will. But the person is only minimally bound to conform to the divine will in the particular matters that are unknown. This is noticeably so with the precepts where this divine will has not been made manifest to him. Fr. Gonet states this more clearly: "A human person is not bound to conform oneself to the divine will in what is materially willed, but only when the divine will is made known to us through a precept or a prohibition."[220] In doubt, therefore, when we do not know whether God has imposed some particular thing on us or has forbidden it, we are not bound to conform ourselves to such a precept of the divine will unless the precept has been made known to us. In fact, as Jean Gerson teaches, where God has not made known his will he cannot, Gerson insists, oblige us to follow it. We repeat his words here, already given above:

> It is necessary that the ordinance and will of God be made manifest, since God, by his ordinance alone or only through his will, cannot impose obligation on a human being in an absolute way.[221]

Saint Thomas confirms this view more strongly in another place where he is specifically talking about the obedience due to divine precepts. His question is *whether God should be obeyed in all things,* which he answers in the affirmative, but then he objects to himself:

> Anyone who obeys God matches his will to God's even in regard to the matter willed...but our will cannot be conformed to the divine will as to the object willed, as we pointed out. Therefore, a human being does not have to give obedience to God in every case.[222]

He answers his own question in the following manner (pay attention to how the holy doctor was always steadfast and consistent in his opinion about this):

> To the third point it is to be said that even though a person is not always bound to do the same thing that God wills, he is bound to will what God wants him to will. And this is principally [note the word] made known by divine precept.[223]

Therefore, the human person is always obliged to obey God, and to conform his will to God's will as regards precepts, but not in regard to all the things that God wills, but only in those things which God wishes us to will *(quod Deus vult eum velle)*. And how can we know not only what God himself wills, but what he wishes us to will too? We know it, says St. Thomas, when it is made obvious to us through his divine precepts: "This is principally made known to a person through divine precept." Therefore, an awareness of a precept that is only doubtful does not oblige one to observe it as if it were the divine will. Certain and manifest knowledge of the precept is required, which is what the word "made known" *(innotescit)* precisely means. Thus, where two opinions of equal weight are present, a sufficient promulgation of the law is lacking in that case and it does not have the power to oblige us. That is what we said at the beginning of this system. A law that does not oblige is not a "law"; *the word comes from* ligando ["binding"] *because it is binding on how we should act.* A law, therefore, that does not bind cannot be called a law.

ARTICLE 60
A precept that is, strictly speaking, doubtful is not obligatory

Authors of older and recent schools commonly follow this opinion: there is no obligation to observe a precept that is, in the proper sense, really doubtful. T. Raymond wrote: "You are not to be too inclined to judge sins as mortal sins when they are not established as certain by Scripture."[224] Lactantius wrote: "It is a very stupid person who wishes to obey precepts which he doubts are either true or false." The text is found in *Cum in iure. De officio et potestate. Judicis delegate. Can. 31:* "Unless you consider the order to be certain, you are not to consider it as being commanded."[225]

John Nider, citing Bernard of Clairvaux, writes in a similar way: "Where there are various opinions among the most learned doctors, and the Church has not decided in favor of one of them, you may hold what you prefer."[226] St. Antoninus gives a comparable view:

> According to the Chancellor [John Gerson], it does no more harm to a person to err about an article of faith, which is not yet declared by the Church as an article to be necessarily believed, than it would be harmful to actually perform a moral act against something. The reason is that the act has not been declared illicit from the Scriptures or by the decision of the Church....In a matter of faith about which the doctors of theology express contrary views, it is licit to hold one view or the other without fear of sinning, until such time as the Church settles the matter...thus, similarly, it is licit to hold an opinion in moral matters, *within the above limits, where at least the wiser doctors have not expressed a contrary view.*[227]

Thus, according to St. Antoninus and the chancellor (that is, Gerson), we are not bound to follow the safer opinion where this opinion does not appear more probable. Gabriel Biel wrote: "Nothing should be denounced as a mortal sin when there is not an evident reason for it, or the verifiable authority of Scripture."[228]

Dominic Soto writes that law, since it is the rule of actions, must be clearly *considered* as such by the person. This means that the person knows that the rule is certain: "Whoever uses a rule must clearly grasp it."[229] He writes later: "When there are probable opinions among the important Doctors, you can follow any one of them and have your conscience at peace."[230] Also, Cardinal

Lambertini (who was afterward elevated to the papacy as Benedict XIV) wrote in his *Notifications*: "You should not impose burdens when there is not a clear law that imposes them."[231]

The very learned Melchior Cano, writing against Scotus who compelled penitents to express contrition on every feast day, writes: "There is neither a human nor an evangelical law by which this precept is asserted: let them produce one, and we will be silent." This is what Cano writes: "Because I do not know how those doctors have arrived at that opinion, I can freely say, without any fear of being contradicted, that the precept has not been sufficiently investigated in a way that can be known."[232]

Joseph Rocafull, the Provost of Valentia, adds: "In a case where, after due diligence, it is not established that the law has been imposed...but remains doubtful, it does not oblige, whether it is a law or a natural precept."[233] Fr. Suarez comments:

> As long as there is a probable judgment that no law exists prohibiting or commanding an action, that law has not been sufficiently proposed or promulgated to a person: therefore, since obligation is of itself burdensome...there is no reason [to follow it] until one becomes more certain about it.[234]

Fr. John Ildephonsus, a Dominican, writes in the similar fashion:

> When there is doubt about the existence or substance of a law, or whether there is indeed such a law, whether it has been published, or whether under such a law this case is covered: if, after due research, the doubt remains, we are not obliged to follow the law.[235]

The same view is held by a recent author, Fr. Eusebius Amort, a very erudite German who is widely known for his teaching and many published works. This is what he says in his moral and scholastic theology, printed at Bologna in 1753 (and which, prior to publication, was amended or at least reviewed by Pope Benedict XIV, as requested by the author himself in a petition that he sent):

> Whenever the existence of a law has not been demonstrated as more credible, it is not itself so morally certain that it can be issued as law. That is clear from the nature of Divine Providence which…is obliged to make its law notably more credible, etc.[236]

Elsewhere, he says that, when there are two opinions of equal probability:

> It is morally certain that a directly prohibitive law cannot be taken from this…because, in this case, a sufficient promulgation of the law is not present, whereas such promulgation is an inseparable and essential character of a law.[237]

The same view is held by Vasquez,[238] Cardinal de Lugo,[239] Mastrius,[240] Holzmann,[241] Roncaglia,[242] the Salmanticenses,[243] and many others whom we omit for the sake of brevity.

ARTICLE 61
Conclusion

The principle handed down from St. Thomas and proven adequately above, namely, that *no one is bound by any precept unless through the knowledge of that precept* is the same as saying that an uncertain law cannot impose a certain obligation.

It is necessary to clearly show how it is morally certain that, when two opinions of equal weight make the same claim, there is no obligation to follow the safer one. If someone requests the reason for the certainty of this view, the answer is briefly stated from all that has been proven up to this point; a doubtful law does not oblige. And if he pursues his inquiry as to why a doubtful law does not oblige, this concise argument is our response. A doubtful law is not sufficiently promulgated; a law that is not sufficiently promulgated does not oblige. (As long as a law is doubtful, it is only the doubt or query that is promulgated adequately, but what is promulgated is not a law.) Therefore, a doubtful law does not oblige. Should anyone wish to refute this explanation, he must be in a position to prove either that a nonpromulgated law does actually oblige, or that a doubtful law is truly promulgated. But this is expressly against what St. Thomas and others customarily teach, as we have seen. Neither of these propositions could ever be proven.

This, then, is the conclusion to this way of thinking. Having considered the equal value of both opinions, the person remains in doubt; hence, he may not act. However, considering the proper value to be given to law, since in this case the law has not been sufficiently promulgated, the law neither obliges nor binds. Thus, since he is not bound by such a doubtful law, the certainty of liberty is restored and, with this liberty, he can lawfully act.

It is clear also from the natural dictate of reason that we can lawfully act in those matters that are not forbidden by law, as Heinneccius writes:

> God permits everything to human liberty that is not commanded or prohibited. Thus, for example, after being prohibited to take the fruits from the tree of the knowledge of good and evil [Genesis 3:2] our first parents could legitimately infer that it was licit to eat the fruits from the other trees. When an obligation of the law is not present, liberty is in possession.[244]

Again, this can be proven in a very valid way from texts of civil and canon law: "It is lawful for anyone to act except where something is prohibited by force of law."[245] "Unless you are certain about the existence of a command, you are not to think that you have to do what is commanded."[246] For this reason, St. Thomas teaches that this is to be held as a common and certain axiom in the natural law. This is what he writes: "Something is to be called lawful which no law prohibits."[247]

There is one or other author who is foolishly arguing: *when there is a doubt about the existence of the law, there is a doubt also about the existence of liberty.* This argument is wrong, in my view. In fact, when there is a doubt whether the law exists, it is certain that the law does not oblige. Saint Thomas noted, as we saw above, that *no one is bound by any precept except through the knowledge of that precept.* It is clear that knowledge means recognition of the law with certainty. The reason for this is evident. Law, as long as there is a doubt, is not sufficiently promulgated; and a law not sufficiently promulgated does not have the power to bind or oblige, as the angelic doctor said in the passages cited above. Where there is not a law capable of binding or prohibiting, a person acts with freedom in a lawful manner, as the same St. Thomas says.[248]

ARTICLE 62
An objection

I said at the beginning that when the opinion in favor of the law appears certainly more probable, then we are bound to follow it; otherwise, it would simply have the same weight as the opinion in favor of liberty. An author of a French journal has objected to me that this proposition tries to prove too much. If we are not bound to follow the opinion in favor of the law, when the opinion in favor of liberty is of equal worth, it implies that the law is doubtful. Therefore, we should not be bound to follow the opinion favoring the more probable law. Even if the opinion in favor of liberty is less probable, a less probable opinion has the effect that the law is doubtful and, thus, the law is not properly promulgated.

My answer is that, although this means that the safer opinion favoring the law is indeed the more probable, however (as outlined in the premise at the beginning of this chapter on our system) the law is not certain. Nevertheless, on account of its greater probability, the opinion in favor of the law appears to be morally more correct and consequently it appears morally and sufficiently promulgated. One cannot say that it is entirely doubtful in the strict sense. All that remains is simply a doubt in the broad sense, which does not permit one to abandon the safer view. If, however, the opinion in favor of liberty is of equal weight, then there is a precise doubt about the existence of the law. Consequently, as we proved, there is no obligation of holding to the stricter opinion or of following the law, about which one entirely doubts whether that law exists or not.

ARTICLE 63
Further objections

Before I conclude this dissertation, I do not wish to omit giving an answer to two opposing views which are expounded by Fr. Flavianus Ricci in the moral theology of Fr. Anacletus—which he himself very recently revised[249]—where he states: all divine and human laws are certain and sufficiently promulgated. The dispute, then, is neither about the existence of the law nor its promulgation. It is about the extent of its application, that is, whether in a particular case we ought to apply the law and investigate whether the case is covered by the law or not. From this we are incorrectly interpreted to be implying that, in the juxtaposition of two opinions of equal weight, we are judging that a certain law does not apply to that case. The author thus presupposes that two things occur in such a case. *Firstly,* that in this case it is our liberty that becomes doubtful and *secondly* that the rule of the canons which should be applied is the one that says *in doubts the safer way is to be chosen.* He adds that this is what Scripture says: "Whoever loves danger will die in the danger" (Ecclesiasticus 3:27).

I respond to the *first objection.* When there is doubt whether a case is to be considered under a particular law or not, we are by no means saying that the law certainly does not apply. What we are saying is that, in the case of two opinions of equal weight, any general law (for example, do not steal, do not kill) certainly exists and is sufficiently promulgated. With respect to its application to this particular case, however, there is doubt, both as regards its existence and its promulgation. Since what is doubted is whether the law is to be extended to that case, it is certain that its obligation cannot be extended to the case. As we proved extensively above, in the case when the law is doubtful, it is impossible for it to bind the freedom the person certainly possesses which, until it is constrained by law, remains free. That indeed is what St. Thomas acknowledged when he says that law is similar to being bound; that is, as long as something is applied to something else by contact, it has the *power of opposing other things.* These are the words of the holy doctor. It is from this that he proposes the judgment: "No one is bound by any precept except through the knowledge of that precept."[250]

This is confirmed elsewhere by St. Thomas in the most robust way, where he writes:

> Law is a kind of rule or measure for human activity through which a person is led to do something or is held back from it. The word comes from *ligando* ["binding"] because it is binding on how we should act.[251]

"A measure," adds Cardinal Gotti, "in order to properly measure, must be applied to the thing to be measured." Then he adds that "law, so that it may bind in action, must be imposed on the subjects by promulgation."[252] How then could a person properly measure his action except by a measure that is itself sure and unambiguous? It is also not correct to say that, where the law is doubtful, the freedom of the person is also doubtful. Freedom always remains certain until that point where it is bound by a law that is equally certain and manifest. Whenever, therefore, there is a certain general law, it certainly exists and it is certainly and sufficiently promulgated. However, as long as the law is not applied to a particular case, freedom, in so far as it is not yet constrained, remains in possession.

I next reply to the *second point*, namely the canonical rule that Fr. Flavianus introduces. I ask him: Is it certain that the above-mentioned rule includes all speculative doubts or does it only deal with practical doubts or doubts of fact? That indeed is not certain, since the general common position teaches that the rule has its place only in practical doubts and in doubts of fact. Here is what St. Antoninus writes:

> Those who wish to prove that a contract is illicit introduce this point: "In doubts the safer way is to be chosen." The response is that it applies to the honesty and the greater part of the merits of the case, but not to every doubt regarding the necessity for salvation: otherwise it would be necessary that everyone enter the consecrated life.[253]

Christianus Lupus[254] makes the same point, arguing it from the doctrine of St. Augustine. The same view is followed by Navarrus, Dominic Soto, Abbas, Nider, Tabiena, Suarez, Angles, St. Bonaventure, Gerson, Ysambertus, John Ildephonsus, Salas, Cornejo, John of St. Thomas, and others. The opinions of all these people can be consulted in a dissertation which I wrote in a more extensive way on this matter.[255] There I clearly proved that this type of canonical rule applies only to practical cases and those of fact. At least the rule or canonical law mentioned is clearly doubtful in any cases beyond practical ones and those of fact. It is thus not sufficiently promulgated and, as a result, does not have the force of obligation.

Suppose we grant without proof that this law applies to all doubts. I ask again: What does this law or rule really say? *In doubts, the safer way is to be chosen.* Therefore, when a person is in doubt, he cannot act. But what if he forms for himself a command that is morally certain about the integrity of his action? Then he is not *in doubt.* He is beyond doubt and outside the canonical rule, as a result of the principle which has been more than sufficiently proven: a doubtful law does not oblige because it lacks the promulgation that is of the essence of law.

The text adds: "Who loves danger will perish in that danger." I cannot understand how this text can favor the above opinion. I am aware of the fact that this verse of Scripture is quoted by all who support the strict view. But I am unable to understand how these masters (as they claim themselves to be) can draw from this text such sober and purer doctrine. The context of Scripture should be noted, where it is said: "A hard heart shall fear evil at the last: and he that loves danger shall perish in it" (Ecclesiastes 3:27). The sense of this section of Scripture is that when a person sins gravely, he puts himself in real danger of his salvation by delaying his conversion until death. In the same way, a person encounters a true danger and sins gravely if he does not voluntarily remove a proximate occasion of sin. This case is totally different from ours in which, given that a doubtful law does not bind, there is no danger of transgressing the law. In this case, the law is not sufficiently promulgated and has no power to impose an obligation.

This is taken from the doctrine of St. Thomas, namely, that the law has no power to oblige unless it is promulgated and made known. Two corollaries arise from what has been said. They are more substantially explained in our *Dissertation* mentioned above.[256] The *first* is that a doubtful law does not oblige and the *second* is connected with this: an uncertain law cannot impose a certain obligation.

FIRST COROLLARY ARTICLES

A Doubtful Law Does Not Bind

ARTICLE 64
A doubtful law does not bind

It is from the principle that a law that is not promulgated does not have the power of obligation, convincingly and frequently proven by St. Thomas, that we derive our first conclusion; *a doubtful law does not oblige.* A conclusion of this type is confirmed by what is taught as certain and generally confirmed among all doctors of theology. The moral certitude of a particular judgment, if not proven by some *direct* principle, can however be proven by some *reflex* principle that is equally certain. This is demonstrated, in the first place, from *Can. 4 Quid culpatur, 23, q. 1* where St. Augustine writes:

> A righteous man, serving perhaps under a degenerate king, may do his duty because he is under orders to do so. In some cases, it is plainly the will of God that he should fight: in other cases, where it is not so clear, it may be an unrighteous command on the part of the king, though the soldier is innocent because his position makes obedience a duty. [257]

Although the subject may have doubts about the justice of the war, can he lawfully go to battle by order of the prince, and on what justification? Sustaining himself by a reflex principle, that the prince has a definite right to give commands, he may obey him. This is equally proved by the chapter *Dominus, de Secundis Nuptiis,* where it is said that if a man is in doubt about the death of the first husband of his wife, he cannot petition the marital debt but he is obliged to render the debt to the wife. She has no doubts, and asks in good faith. Why is this allowable? On the definite reflex principle that, since the wife is in good faith, she has the right to petition the marital debt even if there is doubt on the husband's part.[258]

ARTICLE 65
Two misleading principles of the probabilists

This doctrine is held as certain by Fr. John Lawrence Berti,[259] who says that it is unlawful to follow a less safe opinion, even if it may be equally probable. How does he prove this? He proves it by the falsity of two principles that the probabilists hold to be acceptable. The first of these principles is: *the person who acts with probability acts prudently.* What Berti says, properly and correctly, is that this principle is not a sufficient basis to act with, being an opinion that is merely probable. Since the contrary opinion in favor of the law is equally probable, the certainty of the uprightness of the action is then not sufficient. The second principle of these probabilists is: *when each opinion is probable, a person can suspend judgment on the safer opinion and, basing himself on the probability of the benign view, act accordingly.* Quite correctly, Fr. Berti also rejects this principle. That principle would in no way give the possibility of having certainty about the goodness of our action. The suspension of this type of judgment is purely voluntary. Therefore, it cannot be used as an excuse because the ignorance can be overcome.

Fr. Berti concludes: granted that there is no other basis to dispose of the doubt, other than the simple probability of the benign opinion, then we could only make minimal use of this opinion. Otherwise it would be true, writes Berti, that besides that probability of opinion, some other reflex reason or certain principle could present itself that would make us morally certain of the action in practice.

It could be that the certainty of our judgment would not be dependent on reasons adduced from a probable opinion, but would rest on a definite reflex principle that would then come into use. He offers the example of the religious who doubts whether he could be freed from fasting so he could devote himself to study. This case could be solved if an instruction of the superior points in this direction. He could then be certain that he could take food without guilt. He gives another example. An owner who, possessing a property in good faith, becomes doubtful whether he can lawfully continue with the ownership. A learned person is correctly reported as saying that no one, in doubt, is legitimately bound to deprive himself of a possession. From this he concludes: "Undoubtedly, in this way, on the basis of the reflection of a mind that was previously perplexed, a person could form a judgment that would be morally certain as a practical judgment."[260]

In the same way, Fr. Wigandt of the Order of Preachers writes: "It is probable that it is not a sin to act with a speculatively doubtful conscience, if one combines this with a practical judgment about the goodness of the action."[261] The reason is that the person who acts in this way makes a prudent judgment that, in these circumstances, he can lawfully and honestly act.

There is agreement about this by authors in the work of the master Ballerini, *Rule for the morality of actions or the question of the probable opinion.*[262] Even though actively supporting the rigid opinion, they freely subscribe to this doctrine. *What in practice is derived from direct principles that are minimally certain can, from a reflex principle that is certain, become entirely certain.* In all, they give many examples, especially the one we quoted above regarding the doubtful impediment in a contracted marriage. In this case, they add, given that the matter is uncertain at the level of direct principles (that is, whether a spouse in doubt can ask for the marital debt), nevertheless, a reflex principle, which is deduced from the canons and from reason, makes the matter secure. Hence, they conclude:

> In all these examples it is to be observed that reflex principles are not in a position to resolve a particular question, but they leave one in uncertainty....Only practice is certain, because the reflex principles teach how to establish a certain rule of action when in doubt.[263]

Fr. Gonet shares this view.[264] Indeed, even the lector Fr. John Vincent Patuzzi, who in pamphlets twice strenuously opposed me in this controversy, has come out in favor of my research. He admits, in fact, that when a reflex principle is certain, it confers a definite goodness to the action. He writes in the pamphlet:

> If it were true that in the case of uncertainty of the law, there was then no law, because not sufficiently promulgated: then, yes (as you allude to) you would need to have a certain principle, if not direct, at least a reflex one. From this you could form a prudently certain dictate to allow you to act lawfully [he is talking about some dubiously licit contract] so much so that, there being no law which prohibits it, what reasonable fear could there be about transgressing a law that certainly does not exist?[265]

Better had he said: which *certainly does not oblige* because all the other aspects are reduced to the same point: a law that does not oblige is the same as if there were no law.

In this way, you understand how a speculatively doubtful judgment or probable judgment about the goodness of an action could, in practice, become morally certain. But there will be someone who objects: How can reasons that at the speculative level are only probable turn out to be morally certain in practice? This can happen, as very well explained by Bishop Abelly and Fr. Eusebius Amort. It is not from the fact that the same speculative reasons turn into moral certainty in practice through some opinion or other. It is because there are other reasons for the same opinion that are at least probable, and some others that are true from reflex principles. From these, in practice, the final morally certain judgment is formed from that certain principle. Thus, an action which speculatively is only probably good becomes certainly morally good in practice.

ARTICLE 66
Proof from authority

In order to support our conclusion that a doubtful law does not oblige, we will argue in a clear-cut way. The principle has already been demonstrated above by St. Thomas: a law does not have the power of obligation unless it has been sufficiently promulgated and made known. In the case where two opinions of equal weight clash, therefore, it cannot be said that the law has been sufficiently promulgated. What can be said to be promulgated is a doubt as to whether the law exists, but the law (as law) has not been promulgated. Consequently, that law cannot oblige.

The German, Eusebius Amort, a man well known everywhere for his learning, defended this view as certain in a recently published book (1753) in Bologna on moral and scholastic theology. It was published after it had been corrected in Rome by order of Benedict XIV. The author had petitioned the Pope that, before publication, the work should be revised by prudent theologians in Rome and, where deemed necessary, that it should be amended. The Pope gave his assent and pointed out some defects in the work that needed to be corrected, without touching on the question of the equally probable opinion. This is clear in the published work itself. The author writes that where an opinion in favor of the law is not evidently and noticeably more probable, it is morally certain that an obligatory law does not exist. He says that if God, in accordance with his divine providence, had himself wished his law to oblige, he would have been bound to show that the law was evidently and notably more probable. Here are his words:

> When any time the existence of a law is not itself made more credible, then it is morally certain that this does not create a law. This is clear from the nature of divine providence which is bound to make evident the greater credibility of its own religion or its greater probability, in the same way as it is bound to show that its law is notably more probable.[266]

Saying *not itself (non ipsa)* means, not the law itself, but refers to the reasons which make it notably more probable for us.

Afterward, in another place, he adds a further argument. In the precise sense, because a doubtful law lacks sufficient promulgation, without which there is no law, it is not a law that it is binding. "In that case [namely, each opinion is equally binding] it is morally certain that a direct prohibition cannot be ascribed to the law...[because] in this case there is not sufficient promulgation of the law. Such promulgation is an inseparable and essential character of law."[267] He adds that the Fathers understood the matter in the same way:

> In a doubt strictly so called, when the judgment of the mind is not disposed toward either part, the Fathers leave the person with the power of following the more benign opinions. Therefore, they recognize some general principle by which a person can form a prudent judgment by an accompanying or reflex principle about the non-existence of the law.[268]

Correctly, St. Gregory of Nazianzen, talking of a certain Novatius, says:

> And would you then not allow the young widows, despite of the fickleness of their age, to have the power of entering marriage? That Paul would do this there is not the least doubt, and you clearly accept Paul as a master....True, you say, but only in a minimal way after baptism. By what argument do you confirm this? Either prove that such is indeed the case, or, if you cannot, do not condemn it. Because if something is doubtful, humanity and consideration should win out.[269]

Saint Leo says the same:

> As there are some things that cannot be ignored for any reason [such as the precepts of the *Decalogue*, or the forms of the sacraments as the *Glossa* explain], so also there are many things which, either through the necessity of the

times or for considerations of age, ought to be tolerated. This consideration should always be taken into account. In those things that are either doubtful or obscure, what is neither contrary to Gospel precepts nor found to be against the decrees of the holy Fathers can be followed.[270]

He says that *it can be followed:* superiors ought to allow their subjects to follow less rigid opinions when these are neither contrary to the Gospel nor to the doctrine of the Fathers. This is in line with the instruction of Chrysostom: "As regards your own life, be austere; as regards the life of others, be benign."[271] Lactantius is similar: "They are the most stupid of people who wish to subject a person to precepts when there is a doubt as to whether they are true or false."[272]

Saint Augustine concisely confirms all that we have said. "If what is neither against faith nor against good customs is not convincing, [note: *convincing*], it is to be taken in an indifferent way."[273] Any action, therefore, is permitted to us if we are convinced or morally certain that it is not against faith or good customs. Similarly, the holy doctor, writing to Januarius, reproaches those overly timid souls who think they cannot do anything right in the midst of doubts, except what they take as certain from the authority of Scripture or the tradition of the Church or something that is considered useful for correcting a life. Here are his words:

For I have perceived, often with extreme sorrow, many disturbances caused to weak people by the combative obstinacy or superstitious vacillation of some brethren who, in matters of this kind, which do not admit of final decision by the authority of holy Scripture or by the tradition of the universal Church, or by their manifest good influence on customs. It prevents them from reaching a definite conclusion....It all raises such provocative questions that they consider nothing to be right except what they themselves do.[274]

Saint Basil concurs. Speaking about those who think that some oath taken by them was invalid, he writes:

To be taken into consideration are both the characteristics of the oath, the words used, and the state of soul in which the oath was made and, especially, what might have been added to the words. If at that point, there is no reason for modifying the matter, everything should be entirely put aside.[275]

He says, therefore, that to the extent they are put aside (or not to be listened to), there is no genuinely benign reason in his favor. Saint Bernard has the same view. Writing in a general way about matters that are disputed on both sides, he says to Hugo of St. Victor: "Where someone is confidently sure in their sense of the matter, because of definite arguments or of not being contested by authority, let him not oppose what he senses about the issue."[276] Thus the holy doctor says that a person can safely proceed following those opinions which are based on a certain opinion or on authority, and which are of such importance that no one would deviate from or oppose them. Saint Bonaventure adds to these ideas, writing about vows from which the pope can dispense. He offers three opinions for discussion and at the end concludes:

Which of the three opinions may be truer, I confess that I do not know. It is sufficient that one can subscribe to any of them...if, however, one wants to accept this last one, it should not be seen to be inconvenient for him.[277]

He does not say that the safer view must be accepted, but that any of the views can be supported and accepted. Let us pay attention, further, to Melchior Cano who, opposing the view of Scotus obliging sinners to make an act of contrition on all feast days, writes: "There is neither a human law, nor a gospel one, by which this precept can be asserted: let them produce such a law and I will be silent."[278] He then adds: "Because I do not know how these doctors come to this opinion, I am free without any doubt to deny it because the precept has not been properly explained and made known."[279]

It seems certain that Scotus was of the same view, where he writes about such an opinion: "When, for the most part, the negative side is the more probable, he who follows the less probable affirmative view does not do so without sin."[280] Therefore, for Scotus, the person who follows the equally probable view does not sin. Cardinal Lambertini, later elected Pope under the name Benedict XIV, writes the same thing, saying: "You should not impose burdens when there is not a clear law which imposes one."[281]

ARTICLE 67
Proof from reason

Let us now move on to consider the *intrinsic reasons* for our argument. For this we take the material from the principles involved, guided as ever by the angelic doctor. Saint Thomas defines the law in this way:

Law is a kind of direction or measure for human activity through which a person is led to do something or is held back from doing it. The word for law *(lex)* comes from *ligando* because it is binding on how we should act.[282]

Saint Thomas then teaches that this rule or measure of law has to be manifestly promulgated to people in a way that subjects are bound to observe it. It is for this reason that he asks the question: "Is promulgation essential to law?"[283] This is how he answers:

> The law is laid on subjects to serve as a rule and measure. This means that it has to be brought to bear on them. Hence, to have binding force, which is an essential property of a law, it has to be applied to the people it is meant to direct. This application comes about when their attention is drawn to it by the fact of promulgation. Hence, this is required for a measure to possess the force of law.[284]

Law, therefore, before its promulgation, does not have the power of obliging. As Gratian writes, they acquire the force of law, and they are properly called laws as such, when they are promulgated.[285] *Laws are instituted when they are promulgated.* Consequently, law is defined by St. Thomas in another place: "Law is an ordinance of reason for the common good made by the authority who has care of the community and it is promulgated."[286] Note the words: *ordinance, promulgation.*

Promulgation is unequivocally necessary for law to be obligatory. This applies not only to human laws but also to divine and natural laws, as the same holy doctor teaches. He poses an objection to himself: "Natural law...which is law in the fullest sense of the word, needs no promulgation: therefore, it is not of the essence of law that it be promulgated."[287]

He answers in this way: "Natural law is promulgated by God by so instilling into people's minds so that they can know it naturally."[288]

Thus, St. Thomas does not deny that natural law needs to be promulgated. He says only that this does not happen in a merely human way but through a natural light which God imparts to the human mind. On this point, the most learned Cardinal Gotti says: "So that the law obliges in a second act...it is required without exception that it be promulgated to the subjects."[289] He says: *in a second act,* because law that is not yet promulgated has in itself only the potential of obligation in a first act. To become obligatory, it needs without any exception that its promulgation be made known to the subjects.

Silvius comments: "In reality the law is promulgated for someone when a person comes to know it from God through a dictate of conscience, according to right natural reason, what is to be done and what is to be avoided."[290]

Dominic Soto gives the reason for the necessity of promulgation, so that a law may oblige:

No law has any power of obligation before promulgation... this conclusion allows for no exception and is proven by the nature of law itself. It is the measure and rule of our actions. A rule, unless it is applied to actions, is useless. It cannot be applied, except through notification about it. For a person to use a rule, it is necessary that they have considered it [note: *considered*]. It is, therefore, a consequence that, before promulgation by which it is made known to the subjects, it cannot constrain them through obligation. This can only happen when it is promulgated.[291]

Hence, Jean Gerson says, not even God can compel a human to observe a law unless it has previously been clearly made known by God to the human person as a precept and as his will: "It is necessary to make known the dictate and will of God, as by his will alone it is absolutely not possible for God to impose obligations on a human person."[292] *For this to happen, it is necessary that knowledge of the one and the other should be communicated.* From this, Fr. Gonet deduces the argument that it could well be possible that there is invincible ignorance even of those precepts of the natural precepts that are very distant from the first principles. He argues in this way:

> Law does not have the power of obligation unless it is applied to humans by promulgation or indication....However, the natural law is neither indicated nor communicated to all people regarding all the precepts that it contains, especially as regards those that are most remote from the first principles....Therefore, it does not oblige all humans in regard to those precepts. Consequently, there can be invincible ignorance about these which excuse one from sin.[293]

ARTICLE 68
A first objection and response

We now proceed to the objections of Fr. Patuzzi, from which the certainty of our principles will emerge more clearly explained. Fr. Patuzzi makes a first objection against this principle. To represent a law as sufficiently promulgated, it is enough that we have probable information about it which, on the basis of the probable opinion favoring the law, we already have.

To this objection I make a first reply. The word *notice (notitia)* is the same as *knowledge (cognitio).* Knowledge of the law and a probable opinion about the law are completely different. Besides, I answer, if one wishes that by the word *notice* one means *probable* notification, at most this can be allowed in the case where there is probable information only about the law. Then, indeed, some moral certitude comes to support the law. However, as there is, on the other side, an equally probable opinion in favor of liberty, then on neither side can it be said that the level of probability is more present, or that there is probable reason appropriate for the prudent assent of a person to rely on.

Thus, from these equal probabilities, nothing more than a plain doubt emerges, whether the law exists or not. This is the clear teaching of St. Thomas:

> Our intellect…has a different way of looking at parts of a contradiction: at times it is not inclined toward one more than to the other through lack of motivation as in those problems in which we do not find reasons, or for the apparent equality of motives in favor of one or the other. This is the disposition of one who is in doubt, who fluctuates between the two sides of a contradiction.[294]

He teaches the same thing, more briefly, in another place: "Between equality of reasons and arguments, then, the only place is doubt."[295]

Besides, Fr. Berti says that just as the scale remains equally balanced when no weight is put on it, it is the same way when equal weights are placed on it. In this way, when two probable opinions are placed together on the scales, they thus suspend judgment. From neither side is there probability. "The scale remains in equilibrium, whether no weight is put on either side, or whether on both sides an equal weight is placed."[296]

Fr. Gonet, Vasquez, and Lacroix say the same thing, and generally speaking, so do all probabilists. Finally, Fr. Patuzzi expresses the same view, in these words: "The balance remains steady, in which both scales are assigned a similar weight: the scale does not move to one side or the other."[297] He confirms this elsewhere: "Being obvious that two opinions are contradictory, or equally probable, they cannot but generate doubt."[298]

Thus, in respect to our dispute, in which the question is about two equally probable opinions, it is not enough to say that the probable notification is sufficient to affirm that the law has been sufficiently promulgated. In that case, notification is in no way sufficient to have a promulgated law. What is promulgated is a doubt or a simple hesitation as to whether there is a law or not. When all is said and done, if two opinions of equal weight are in competition, the result is, as we said, that neither of them carries weight.

<h1 style="text-align:center">ARTICLE 69</h1>

A second objection and response

Patuzzi has a second objection. The promulgation of law is one thing, another is its being published or the private information which the subjects receive about it. The law, as it had already been promulgated, has the power of obligation, even without the information having been received by the subjects. The law obliges because all laws, whether human or divine, are already sufficiently promulgated. Speaking in the first place *about human laws,* he says that for these to be binding it is sufficient that they be either promulgated to the community by public announcers, or be placed as written notices in public places.

We concede that, for a human law to have the power of obligation, it is sufficient that it be promulgated to the community. It is not required that the information reach each and every subject. To be noted, however, is that this holds only for the material object of the law, that which is allowed or forbidden by the law. It does not hold as regards observing the law in conscience.

Let me explain myself, with an example. If a law has been promulgated by which an invalid contract had been entered into without the usual formalities; then, the subject is bound by the prescript of the designated law as soon as he is notified about it, even if he had been ignorant of its existence. The contract is then considered to have no effect. Otherwise, the person will have to accept the appropriate penalty since, in the external forum, once a law is promulgated, all are presumed to know about it.

In respect of conscience, however, surely a person sins negligibly when he does not observe a law that was unknown to him. This is so, unless it was the case that he did not know the law on account of his own negligence. It is in this way that the text from St. Thomas, quoted by Patuzzi, is to be understood: "Those who are not present when a law is promulgated are obliged to observance in that, given the fact of promulgation, the law is or can be brought to their attention by others."[299]

This "can be brought to their attention" is to be understood insofar as notice about the law could have reached the subject but, due to their carelessness, it did not. However, if their ignorance is not culpable, they sin negligibly by not observing the law. Cajetan correctly mentions the fact that only those are to be held guilty of an offense against the law if they do not know about it.

> This happens either because they did not wish to know it or because they neglected to do what was necessary in order to know it. Otherwise, people who were absent and thus ignorant of the law cannot be bound by the law. On that account…they cannot be accused before man or God on account of ignorance.[300]

This is the same as what Peter Collet[301] and Fr. Franciscus Suarez[302] write. A similar point is added by Fr. Suarez,[303] Aravius,[304]

Tapia,[305] Castropalaus,[306] Gregorius Martinez,[307] Sanchez,[308] Villalobos,[309] and the Salmanticenses.[310] Not only are such people to be considered as ignorant in not knowing the law, but also those who, after due diligence, are in doubt about the law. As we have said, the law does not bind unless it is applicable to subjects as a law that is certain, and not only as a doubtful report. This is what has been handed on to us by the same St. Thomas who teaches: "No one is bound by any precept unless through the knowledge of that precept."[311] This text will be discussed further on.

ARTICLE 70
A third objection and response

So much for human laws. Speaking, however, *of divine laws,* Patuzzi claims that these have been promulgated from eternity and so, from eternity, have the complete power of binding before human beings would have heard of them or known about them. He says that this ensues from the fact that the eternal law has, from eternity, causal, virtual, and notable promulgation. Thus, in time (that is, outside eternity) they have a formal promulgation. He infers this from the words of St. Thomas:

> Promulgation is made by word or writing: in both ways, an Eternal Law is proclaimed by God's utterance, since the Divine Word and the Book of Life are eternal. Admittedly, on the side of the creature who listens to or reads this, the promulgation cannot be from all eternity.[312]

Nevertheless, I assert that eternal law, with respect to humans, is not properly called law. Law for humans, correctly speaking, is the natural law. Even though it participates in the eternal law, it is still as natural law that it properly binds people, in the proper sense. It is only the natural law which is promulgated to humans and it is to be applied through the light of reason. At the very least, I say (just as other authors affirm) that the eternal law, even though it has the power of obligation at the first level of the first act (potentially), nevertheless it is not law that obliges in reality and at the second level of application (actually). It has to be proposed, and through knowledge of it, is then applicable to humans. I affirm that such is what is taught by St. Thomas and by all theologians. Consider how Duvallius speaks of the matter.

> Finally, can you doubt whether that eternal law always had, and still has, the true and proper meaning of law? I answer: in time, when creatures appear, it has in fact the meaning of true law when it is indeed truly and properly imparted to and imposed on all human creatures as subjects of the law. If, however, it is looked at from the perspective of eternity it has to be said that it is not truly and properly law but only something that has the appearance of law.[313]

He then explains the reason:

> For law to have the real meaning of law, it has to be imposed on and promulgated to subjects: no one was a subject from eternity....Thus, since law in this world is essentially some sort of practical rule, this cannot be imposed on the Word and the Holy Spirit because they, in themselves, are law and righteousness itself.[314]

Peter de Lorca writes similarly.

The eternal law is not the principle or the reason of the action of anyone who might be subject to the law, nor is it the proximate rule of human actions. It is the reason of action for God himself, and the rule of divine operations by which he governs the world. If there is a law, it is because there is a God...if, in this way, the eternal law considers humans, it does so in a remote way, insofar as one is moved and governed by God, not simply because God has his rule extended over creatures as if he proposed this to them as a rule by which they could measure and arrange their actions.[315]

Speaking of these remarks of St. Thomas, he comments on "and in word":

That expression "in the divine word" was eternal and was made in the nature of God by the necessity of his nature. It is not related to any human creatures which requires the promulgation of law: promulgation of law is always in reference to its promulgation to subjects.[316]

Ludovicus Montesimus writes in the same way:

I respond that the eternal law of this type is promulgated from eternity to God himself: God is the law unto himself, and he is the measure of that law. Thus, we understand that God promulgated the law for himself.[317]

Speaking of the eternal law, Lorichius writes in the same way:

> By this law God has ordered everything to himself...it is promulgated to himself from eternity...but to humans it is promulgated when it is made known to them and remains known.[318]

How can these doctrines be in any way reconciled with what Fr. Patuzzi says, namely, that the eternal law had the full power of obliging humans, from eternity itself, before human creatures had heard or knew about the law? From these teachings taken from others, there is similarity with what St. Thomas says in another place. He asserts that the eternal law is not the proximate law of the human will, but rather it expresses the *mind of God*. Here are his words:

> The human will is subject to a twofold rule: one is proximate and on his own level, that is, human reason: the other is the first rule beyond man's own level, that is, the eternal law which is the mind of God.[319]

This is not opposed to the words of the same holy doctor, given above: "The eternal law has its promulgation from the side of God promulgating it."[320] In the same place the holy doctor adds: "But from the perspective of the human person listening to or reading, there cannot be a promulgation from eternity."

Now, I ask, what is the promulgation of divine law that binds humans? Promulgation *from the side of God* or *promulgation from the side of human creatures*? This is explained by St. Thomas in the same place:

For law to have the power of obligation…it has to be applied to the people it is meant to direct. This application comes about when their attention is drawn to it by the fact of promulgation.[321]

Then, objecting to himself *at the first point* that the natural law does not need promulgation, he answers that *natural law is promulgated by God, so instilling it into people's minds that they can know it because of who they really are.*

Now I come to my argument. If it were true that St. Thomas believed that eternal law, by the fact that it has eternal promulgation, would oblige people from eternity, even before they knew the law, then for this reason he would have answered that the natural law, which is a participation in the eternal law, would not have needed promulgation. However, he answers that promulgation of the natural law happens when it is made known to people by the light of natural reason. He could not have answered otherwise, since earlier in the same article he states firmly that no law of any kind can have the power of obliging, except insofar as it comes to the notice of people by being understood from promulgation.

Add the point, which St. Thomas treats in another place, where he asks, *is there a natural law within us?* He answers:

It is to be said that…law exists in two manners, first as the thing which is the rule and measure, second as the thing which is ruled and measured….Insofar as something participates in a rule…so is it ruled….And this sharing in the Eternal Law by intelligent human creatures is what we call "natural law."[322]

The holy doctor here distinguishes the eternal law from the natural law. The eternal law concerns God as ruler while the natural law is concerned with humans as the ones ruled. Hence, as the natural law is a participation in the eternal law, thus, *insofar as something participates through the rule* (through natural law) *so is it itself ruled*. Therefore, insofar as the eternal law binds people, it is to the extent that it is participated in by people through the natural law whose promulgation is manifest. This is what Duvallius says:

> You ask…in what way is the eternal law made known to us, which is the same as if it were being asked in what way has it been promulgated…I say that it exists in human creatures insofar as they are subjects, and it becomes known to them through other laws….In fact, these laws participate in it.[323]

The same point is confirmed by Franciscus de Arauxo:

> Since the eternal law does not oblige rational creatures, except through the natural law or through positive divine or human law, it is necessary for their promulgation that these too be sufficiently promulgated.[324]

The law that binds people is only the natural law because it alone can be the rule and measure for a person by which one can be ruled and measured. Besides, although we admit that the eternal law is properly law with regard also to human beings, and that it has potentially the force of binding, what then is the implication? Indeed, the eternal law does not bind at the level of action. This is because it is not promulgated to human creatures, through which knowledge it would be applied. Wisely, Cardinal Gotti conveys this idea:

It follows that the eternal law could bind no one at the level of action, not through a defect of power to do so, but from the lack of a proper point of reference. It is law from eternity conceived in the mind of God, although from eternity it was not promulgated, nor implemented, nor obligatory in an applied action. It is, however, law from eternity, since for the meaning of law it is enough that it has the power of obliging, although it does not yet bind, because it is not yet applied and promulgated.[325]

Let the words be noted: it does not bind because it is not yet applied and promulgated. Tournely Continuator writes in a similar tone:

Because, however, eternal law, before the existence of human creatures, was not obligatory in a strict and true sense, because there was nothing external to which it could impose an obligation, it is obviously true that, to have full and complete meaning as law, it must have human creatures to whom it has been intimated and promulgated. At least it begins to give them order and motivation though its imprint.[326]

Fr. Cuniliati is of the same view: "Those people are not violators of law when the law has not yet been made known."[327] Fr. Patuzzi insists: if the eternal law were truly law, before humans properly knew of it, before the law had been made known to them, it obliges people since it had the essential property of any law, which is to impose an obligation. He quotes Cardinal Gotti as being on his side: the eternal law is truly law, and accordingly has the power of obligation from eternity.

I answer by making a distinction. One thing is the quality of a promulgated law, another is that of a law which is not promulgated. The property of a promulgated law is that it is fully obligatory in actuality. The characteristic of a law that is not promulgated is that it is only imperfectly obligatory in a potential sense. A law that is not promulgated has in itself the intrinsic power of obliging, but only as regards the future, that is: at the time when it has been indicated to humans and has been applied through notification of it. If, in truth, it has not been made applicable, it does not oblige, nor does it have the power of obligation in reality.

As the angelic doctor says: "Hence, to have binding force… it has to be applied to the people it is meant to direct."[328] This is not contrary to what Cardinal Gotti writes, saying that the eternal law, even if not yet promulgated to people, has the power of obligation. Saint Thomas is talking of the actual power of obligation in the performance of an act. Gotti, however, speaks of the power of obligation only in the first potential level. Law, indeed, carries obligation in a potential sense, but in order that law be suitable for obligation in practice, it must be actually promulgated. It does not have this power before promulgation. In a similar way, fire has the power of burning something, but it does not actually burn anything until the fire is applied to the thing to be burnt. Confer, indeed, how the same Cardinal Gotti says the same thing about the eternal law:

And so from eternity the law was conceived in the mind of God, even though it was neither promulgated nor implemented from eternity…In this way, since from eternity there was no human creature whom it could oblige or to whom it could be applied, it does not oblige from the eternal act itself. It is, however, law from eternity because, to have the meaning of law, it is enough that it has the potential power of obligation, even though it does not yet bind because it has not yet been applied or promulgated.[329]

Nor can it be said that the eternal law did not oblige from eternity because of a defect in its point of reference, which is obviously the fact that there were no human creatures from eternity. It is not only that the eternal law did not oblige human creatures from eternity, because the human person did not exist from eternity. There is also the consideration that the law could not oblige in particular reality before it had been actually applied and promulgated. Cardinal Gotti had already said elsewhere that "in order for law to oblige at the level of action it is required, without exception that it be proposed to the subjects by promulgation."[330]

About the same matter, he later wrote, as above, that the eternal law was law from eternity *although it does not yet bind because it has not yet been applied and promulgated.* Continuator Tournely, speaking of eternal law, wrote the same thing, as we saw: "It is entirely clear that the full and complete meaning of law can only consist in this: when there were human creatures to whom it had been indicated and promulgated."[331] Silvius says the same: "In reality [natural law]…is promulgated to someone when a person accepts the knowledge of it from God as a dictate which says, according to right natural reason, that something is to be done or something is to be avoided."[332]

ARTICLE 71
A fourth objection: When is natural law promulgated?

Fr. Patuzzi raises a fourth objection. Natural law is promulgated as a habit since God creates the soul and infuses it into the body, thus imprinting the light of reason in it. From this, Patuzzi infers that the human person is bound by law from conception. Since God imprints the law in the soul, he thus also promulgates it, and in support he refers to the text of St. Thomas: "the promulgation of natural law occurs from the fact that God inserts it into the minds of humans so that it is naturally known."[333]

In answering, it is necessary to scrutinize the mind of St. Thomas in what he says in the main section of the article. There he teaches that law is imposed by reason of a rule and measure when he states that, to have the power of obligation, it is necessary *that it be applied to humans who ought to regulate themselves according to it.* He adds that this *happens through the notification of these laws as understood from the promulgation itself.* According to St. Thomas, therefore, law binds a person when it is applied to them through being notified about it, or through it being made known to them. He says that promulgation of law occurs *from the fact that God inserted it naturally so that it could be known.*

That, undoubtedly, is to be understood in the following way, unless we wish to have the holy doctor contradict himself in the same article. Law is truly promulgated and receives its power of obliging when it is in reality applied and made known. In this regard the angelic doctor says elsewhere: "On the side of the human creature who is hearing or inspecting the law, promulgation cannot be from all eternity."[334]

Therefore, a law is promulgated when a human person either hears about it from the Church or becomes acquainted with it through the light of reason. Hence, Thomas says that the law of nature is "nothing other than the light of natural reason, shining on us, by which we discern what is good and what is evil."[335] This light, however, by which we discern good and evil, and in which the natural law consists, does not display to humans what are the good and evil deeds before a person has the use of reason. Saint Antoninus implies this. Here are his words:

Note with great attention, according to the Blessed Thomas, that the light of the natural law about the goods to choose is not shown to humans until they have reached the use of reason.[336]

Therefore, the natural law is not promulgated to a human person unless he has attained the use of reason. From this, it can be concluded that, properly and strictly speaking, law is not yet given with the infusion of the soul; a light is implanted by which the law can become known by a human person when they reach the use of reason. In other words, the potency, the capacity, and the ability to know the natural law is given at the time of the use of reason. Therefore, when a person knows the law, the law is perfectly and truly promulgated to the person, and it binds him.

Saint Thomas teaches that, until the point that the law has not been brought to the notice of a person through promulgation, the law has not acquired the power of binding. It can be added to this what Dominic Soto writes: "Law cannot be applied except from the notification of the law, for when a person uses a law, it is necessary that the person have his attention drawn to it."[337]

Note also what Jean Gerson said, using these very noteworthy words:

That law [natural law] is a sort of revelation or, properly speaking, a disclosure made to the rational human person, by which the person recognizes what God has judged about certain things, on which God wishes to oblige the human creature, regarding what actions are to be done or to be avoided, so that they would make the human person worthy of eternal life.[338]

To this, having offered a definition of the divine law, he adds:

> It is necessary that a manifestation of the ordinance or will of God be made known, since it is only through his ordinance or his will that God imposes obligations on humans. For this to happen, however, it is necessary that God give notice of the one or the other to the human person. From this, the conclusion can immediately be drawn that a rational creature cannot be considered unworthy of the friendship of God, nor become subject to punishment through sin, unless knowingly, willingly, and freely he performs an action that is prohibited or omits an action that is a precept.[339]

Therefore, according to Gerson, not even God can force the observance of a law on a person unless he first makes it known to the person.

Nor is it damaging to this argument of St. Thomas, who says that the natural law inheres in a person since childhood. The holy doctor himself says in the same passage that law, properly speaking, is an act and not a habit. The reason is that the law consists in the act by which the law is articulated, through the dictate of the reasoning process, which prescribes what is to be done and what is to be avoided. Silvius aptly says:

> Natural law is an act of reason, indeed an actual judgment, and in practice it is a dictate of reason. The argument is that every law becomes such by means of declaration and declaration is a type of an act. The power of obligation is not simply knowledge, insofar as it is this or that knowledge...it comes from the dictate of reason which prescribes those things which, in themselves, are good and

thus to be done, or those things that are prohibited, and in themselves bad, and thus to be avoided.[340]

Cardinal Gotti explains that more at length:

From all of this it is clear that we speak of the natural law as it commands in the second act. This comprises the essence of law, which one understands as something that commands. If we take the natural law [as being] in the first potential level, thus understanding the law as a power and as some sort of habit,...we do not consider the principles in the first instance. The light of reason always remains in the intellect, which God has placed in each rational creature along with his nature. From this, if one uses the power of reason, one can form a judgment and a command about what is to be done and what avoided.[341]

Cardinal Gotti distinguishes the natural law in the first act of potency and in the second act of doing. He says that the natural law, considered in the first act and as a habit, consists in that habitual light of reason that is instilled into us along with our nature. From this light, therefore, the practical dictate is formed after the time that a person reaches the use of reason. However, the natural law, considered in the second level of action, essentially consists in the actual determination of law that is made for the human person in the practical order.

I now ask: Where exactly is the essence of law actually to be found? Is it perhaps inserted into the habit of the law when the soul is created, or is it truly to be found in the actual determination of law itself? Is it only the light that is inserted at the moment of creation that makes the natural law a perfect law, or does this occur with the actual declaration of the law and its intimation?

Gotti affirms (as Silvius did, as we saw above, and others such as St. Thomas, Gerson, Soto, Gonet and more, as we shall see below); the essence of law is not indeed something in the habit of a person but in the actual declaration of the law. We repeat the words of the Cardinal: "It is obvious to us to speak of the natural law as a declaration of a second act, in which the essence of law consists and which it possesses by means of proclamation." From this declaration, there is afterward formed the dictate of reason, obliging a person to (obey) the law.

Silvius is of the same view, following the words of St. Thomas,[342] that the natural law is implanted in a person with the infusion of the soul. In the same place, he acknowledges the difficulty by which, through the habitual insertion of the law, a person could be bound even before the law is made manifest to him in a prior moment. Hence, he adds:

> Thus, it could be said that the natural law could be promulgation in the habit of a person, from the very fact that God imprinted it in the minds of people....But in fact it could only be promulgated when a person accepts from God a dictate that is known according to natural right reason regarding what is to be done and what avoided.[343]

In this way, Silvius calls this first insertion of the law in a human person at conception as a sort of *quasipromulgation* in the habit or disposition of a person. However, he refers to it as promulgation in the absolute sense when it becomes such in reality, that is, when a law is made known to a person as that by which he ought to be regulated. It is certain, therefore, in offering this view, that he means to say that the impression made in a human person, before a person actually comes to know the law, is not sufficient to bind him, and that is why he adds: "and so it must be added."

Afterward he says that actual promulgation occurs when a person accepts the knowledge of the law, because this is the necessary and adequate promulgation through which a person is bound by the law and through which his life is measured. That, without a doubt, is what Silvius thinks, as can be seen from what he writes elsewhere:

> The eternal law was, from eternity, law in the material sense....However, it was not such in a formal sense from eternity or in the notion of a law that was obligatory in reality, because there was not yet actual and perfect promulgation.[344]

Silvius says that eternal law (in the same way as it proceeds from the natural law, which is a participation in the eternal law) is not yet law that is formally and in reality binding, unless an actual promulgation occurs. It is when promulgation occurs that a person discerns what is to be done and what avoided, according to what Silvius himself had previously expressed:

> In reality, then [natural law] is promulgated to someone when they accept the knowledge of it from God as a dictate according to right natural reason about what is to be embraced and what is to be avoided.[345]

The natural law that is not promulgated to a human person does not oblige him, unless the person has reached the use of reason when the law is made known and promulgated to him. Fr. Ludovicus Montesimus says:

> The natural law is promulgated in someone when a person first comes to the use of reason. Although the law is

only promulgated for the most common principles of the natural law, afterward and gradually, the same law is promulgated with regard to the other precepts through life's journey.[346]

Duvallius writes comparably: "You ask at what time does the natural law begin to oblige someone? I respond that it obliges when it is promulgated. Thus, it is sufficiently promulgated when someone reaches the age of discretion."[347] Petrus de Lorca says: "In the way in which promulgation is intrinsic and essential to human laws, so the judgment of reason and intrinsic knowledge is necessary for the natural law."[348] Take note: *judgment and knowledge are intrinsic to law.* Therefore, without judgment and knowledge of the law, the law does not bind. Fr. Cuniliati writes in a comparable vein:

> The violators of law...are not those to whom the law is not yet made known....The actual promulgation of the natural law happens when a person accepts knowledge of the dictate from God as to what, according to natural reason, is to be avoided or held on to.[349]

Similarly, Fr. Gonet:

> The promulgation of the natural law occurs through the dictate of reason: those things are indicated to a person, which are proscribed by the natural law or those that are forbidden. Therefore, when such a dictate is not present, the law of nature does not oblige as regards its observation.[350]

The learned Fr. Mastrius writes in the same way:

This law [of nature] is indicated to people and begins to oblige from the time in which they accept the use of reason. Through such a law indicated to the person, they learn to distinguish between good and evil. For these, indeed, the use of reason is as if it were the notification and manifestation of the natural law itself. *This is what Paul means*: "I used to live at that time when there was no law, but when the commandment came, sin came back too" (Romans 7:9). Jerome explains it in this way: "When...the commandment came, that is the time of understanding, and of desiring good and of avoiding evil, it is then that sin began to come to life again and the time of death for the person guilty of sin."[351, 352]

ARTICLE 72
A fifth objection

Fr. Patuzzi makes a fifth objection:

For a law to be doubtful, there must be a doubt whether such a law exists. This cannot happen since laws, human as well as divine, which we are bound to observe, are all certain and sufficiently promulgated. The doubt that remains, therefore, is not about the existence of the law, but about the particular cases, whether they are to be understood as coming under the universal law or not. If, on the principle proposed, we wish to say that a doubtful law does not bind, we cannot say this on the basis that the law is doubtful because it is not a law. We can only say, since on both sides there is a probable opinion, whether the law applies to these cases or not, then the law cannot certainly be extended to them in such cases. But, if this is said, the difficulty of the principle returns. When it is doubtful whether such an action is lawful or not, in the sense whether it is to be understood as covered by the law, it is not possible to propose such a principle as certain.[353]

Up to this point, Fr. Lector Patuzzi is keeping to what Fr. Daniel Concina had previously written in his theology.[354] As a response, we take what the same Concina writes in the *Compendium*[355] of his theology where he says: it may be that the law is certain, nevertheless there are different circumstances that happen so that sometimes the law obliges and at other times it does not. Precepts, even though they are unchanging, sometimes are not obligatory under this or that circumstance.

Here we summarize the argument. It is not enough to say that the laws are certain, for with the changed circumstances of the case, they are rendered non-obligatory or at least doubtful. Being doubtful, they cannot even be obligatory. Therefore (Fr. Patuzzi might answer), according to your principle that a doubtful law does not oblige, would you conclude that in a doubt whether the law is to be extended to that case or not, certainly it does not apply? We respond by turning the argument around. According to your judgment, in doubt whether the law extends to this case or not, do we certainly have to say that it does extend? This is what we repudiate. We are not asserting at any rate that a doubtful law is definitely not extended to that case. What we say is that, as often as there are equally probable opinions on both sides, when it is not certain that the law applies to that case, then the law is rendered doubtful in respect of that case. Being doubtful, it does not oblige because it has not been sufficiently promulgated.

An example can make the matter clearer. We have a universal law that prohibits usury. However, when on both sides there is a probable opinion whether this particular contract is or is not one of usury, then there is no law that would clearly forbid it. Thus, as long as it is prudently doubted whether it is a proper contract and not one based on usury, although there be an opinion that such a contract is of the type forbidden by law, there is however no certain law that can be applied to it. In respect, therefore, of that particular contract the law is doubtful. With respect to usury, the law prohibiting it is certain; with respect, however, to that particular contract, the law is uncertain. Then why object (as our opponent does) that here one is not dealing with a question of whether the law exists or not, since the law forbidding usury is certain? We are only examining whether the law extends to that case or not. The answer is clear: given that it is truly probable that this case is not covered by the law, there is a doubt whether the law extends to that case. That is to say, the law, because it is doubtful with respect of that case, cannot impose an obligation in that case.

SECOND COROLLARY ARTICLES

Uncertain Law Cannot Impose Certain Obligation

ARTICLE 73
Law ought to be certain

"The law has to be...clearly evident," said St. Isidore.[356] From this, Panormitanus asserts: "Where the law is obviously doubtful, the person ignorant of the law is excused."[357] Natural reason indicates the same point: nobody is obliged to observe those precepts when in doubt whether they exist or not. *In doubt no one is presumed to be obliged.* This is what St. Thomas teaches: law (and here he is speaking of divine and eternal law) must be certain in order to oblige.[358] In the same place, the holy doctor objects to himself:

> A measure should be most certain. Yet we cannot ascertain what the Eternal Law is. Hence, it cannot be the measure which rules the goodness of our act of will....Although as dwelling in the divine mind the Eternal Law is unknown to us, nevertheless in some fashion it becomes known to us either through natural reason, which derives

from the divine mind as its proper image, or through some revelation given to us over and above the powers of reason.[359]

Thomas does not therefore deny that the divine law, insofar as it is the measure of our actions, ought to be certain. As for the issue concerned, he simply affirms that it is not necessary that it be known in the same way by God and by us: it is sufficient that it become known to us either through the light of natural reason or by some special revelation.

This point is outlined even more clearly and powerfully in another place by the angelic master, where he asks: "Does conscience bind?" He answers:

> The command of a ruler binds in voluntary matters—
> with the type of bond that is concerned with the will—as
> a bodily action binds a bodily reality with the necessity
> of force. But the action of a bodily agent never induces
> necessity in something except through contact of the ac-
> tion with the thing on which it acts. Whence [analogical-
> ly] a person is not bound by some lord or master if the
> command does not reach the person to be commanded.
> However, this happens through knowledge. Thus, no one
> is bound by any precept except through the knowledge
> of that precept, and hence the person who has not the ca-
> pacity of knowing the precept cannot be said to be bound
> to fulfill the precept. Nor can a person, ignorant of the
> precept of God, be bound to fulfill that precept except
> insofar as he is bound to come to know that precept. If,
> however, a person is not bound to know it and does not
> know it, that person is in no way bound by the precept.
> As, indeed, in bodily reality the bodily agent does not act

except through contact, so in spiritual matters a precept does not bind except through knowledge.[360]

Take note of that: *no one is bound by some precept except through the knowledge of that precept.*

ARTICLE 74
A first objection and answer

Let us now hear the objections of Fr. Patuzzi to this second principle, specifically in regard to the text of St. Thomas. He objects firstly that the word *knowledge* is not to be understood as certain recognition, but only the simple notification of the principle which (he says) in this case we probably have on account of the probability of both opinions. I answer, by firstly saying that the term *knowledge* is to be understood as probable notification, as in the interpretation given by the most recent dictionaries. Meanwhile all philosophers, St. Thomas among them, distinguish *opinion* from *knowledge*, which is recognized as the certain knowledge of some truth.

Fr. Patuzzi insists that St. Thomas, by the term *knowledge,* understands something that is to be taken as a probable notification, as in the case we are discussing. Patuzzi notes that the angelic doctor then adds: "Thus, he who is not capable of receiving the notification is not bound by the precept." However, by the same token, I say that *notification* has the same meaning as *knowledge.* Therefore, *notification* of the law is the same as *knowledge* of the law. Besides, given that the term *notification* could be understood as the probability of the existence of the law, at most its probability could be conceded in that it stands for the law, with no probability for an opposing view. Otherwise, since an opinion favoring freedom is equally probable, then it is certain (as we say) that nothing takes precedence, except the simple hesitation about the law. This hesitation is neither knowledge nor notification. Therefore, we do not have notification of the law, but only notification of the doubt whether the law exists or not.

What St. Thomas means to say by affirming *through the medium of knowledge* is not something concerning doubts or a disputed opinion, but true knowledge. This is evident from the context of that same article where he says:

> As in bodily matters, the bodily agent does not act except through contact [constraint on the thing, as we said above] so, in spiritual matters, a precept does not bind except through knowledge....To see, however, in what way conscience binds, it is necessary to know that the binding, transferred metaphorically from bodily realities to spiritual realities, brings with it the necessity of an obligation. In fact, he who is bound must necessarily remain in the place where he is bound, and he is deprived of the capability of moving to another place.

Therefore, just as the person who is not actually physically bound, has the power of going in whatever direction he wishes, so the person who is not yet bound by a precept, through knowledge of that precept, has the power of acting as he would choose. In what other way could it be said that someone really knows the precept, if he himself knows the precept to be doubtful? Thus, it is not proper to say that he is ignorant of the precept since he doubts whether the precept exists or not.

Besides, Patuzzi objects, on the basis of the above text and these words: "Nor is someone who is ignorant of the precept of God bound to fulfill the precept, unless insofar as he is bound to know the precept." Thus, Fr. Patuzzi argues, even if someone lacks knowledge of the law, he is bound to seek that knowledge. He is already bound by the precept, and he cannot be excused if he transgresses it. This is a minimalist way to understand what Aquinas teaches. He only says that the person, who knows that he is bound by the law and then culpably ignores it, is not excused from sin. That is clear from what he adds in the same article: "An erroneous conscience is not sufficient in order to be absolved, when the person sins in the error itself." How could the person sin *in the error itself* unless the same error is a sin, on account of a negligent will? Saint Thomas, using St. Augustine, plainly declares in another place:

> Ignorance, which is entirely involuntary, is not a sin, and this is what Augustine says: "You are not regarded as guilty if, unknowingly, you ignore something, but only if you show negligence about knowing it."[361] When he adds "but only if you have neglected to know it," he means to imply that ignorance has the character of sin on the basis of the preceding negligence, which is nothing other than the negligence of the spirit to know what one should know.[362]

Therefore, in no way does a person sin who, hesitating before two opinions of equal probability, seeks out the law and, having shown due diligence, finds it to be completely doubtful and, therefore, not obligatory.

ARTICLE 75
A second objection and answer

Patuzzi makes a second objection. Eternal laws are in position of ownership, and have precedence over our title to liberty. Consequently, he says that, in doubtful matters, the opinion in favor of the law is to be preferred.

Here is my answer: as we saw above, according to what theologians say, the eternal law is not really and truly law in respect of people. Even granted that it was so, in no way can it be said that the eternal law can impose an obligation that is antecedent to the freedom granted by the Lord to people. Although, indeed, in God there is no sequential ordering of knowledge and deliberation, because all things were present to God from eternity, nevertheless, through *the priority of reason or nature* the human person is conceived in the divine mind before the law. Firstly, human persons are considered by the legislator as subjects according to their proper nature and state. Afterward, consideration is given to the law suitable to be imposed on them. I say *suitable*: since God instituted one law for angels, another for humans, one law for priests and one law for laity, another law for married people and yet another for celibate people. This teaching is not mine but that of St. Thomas, who asks the question: "Is there an eternal law?"[363] In the first part, he makes this objection to himself:

> There is no eternal law, it seems. Every law supposes subjects on which it is imposed. Yet there was none such from eternity: God alone is from eternity. Therefore, no law is eternal.[364]

He answers his own objection:

To the first point...it is to be said that while not yet existing in themselves, things nevertheless exist in God, insofar as they are foreseen and preordained by him, according to what Paul speaks (Romans 4:17). God summons things that were not yet in existence as if they already were. Thus, the eternal concept of divine law bears the character of a law that is eternal as being God's arrangement for the governance of the things he foreknows.[365]

Take note: *of the things he foreknows.* Thus, by the *priority of reason,* the human person was first considered by God as free, and only then was significance given to the law by which the human could be bound. To take an example: from eternity God prohibited murder, therefore by the *priority of reason* he first considered people who were capable of murder and afterward he gave the precept that one should not kill another person.

And so, says Fr. Patuzzi, the human person is born free and independent? By no means. The human person is born subject to divine power and, consequently, he is bound to submit to all the precepts which God could impose on him. That a person be bound by precepts of this kind, however, it is necessary that they be promulgated to him and that he knows them through the light of reason. As long as the precept is not made known to a person, he keeps possession of the liberty that God has granted to him. This liberty remains certain unless the person becomes bound by a precept. Because law is the rule and measure by which a person rules and measures one's actions, it is necessary that this rule and measure not be uncertain. What our adversaries claim, therefore, is false; namely, that a person can do nothing unless he knows that this has certainly been permitted by the Lord. If this were so, the divine law would not need promulgation. It would simply be sufficient that God would declare all those things he permits us to do.

However, God did not act like that: "It was he who created man in the beginning, and left him in the power of his own inclination. If you will, you can keep the commandments, and to act faithfully in a matter of your own choice" (Ecclesiasticus 15:14). God first created humans as free, giving freedom to the person as it pleased him, according to what the apostle writes: "having... power over his own will" (1 Corinthians 7:37). Afterward, he ordered and imposed the laws that were meant to be obeyed. Thus, a person first possesses freedom, since it is certain, unless this liberty has been bound by a certain law.

This is what the older authors commonly taught. Where the law is unclear, and to support it there is no clear scriptural text, or decision by the Church, or well-defined argument, then nothing should be condemned as a grave sin. They held it as certain that a doubtful law does not oblige....Raymond writes: "You should not be too inclined to judge sins as mortal when it is not certain to you from sacred Scripture."[366] Saint Antoninus says the same:

> If [the confessor] cannot clearly see whether something is a mortal sin...he should not be seen to give a hasty judgment, as William the Speculator advises in a similar situation: should he absolutely deny absolution on account of this, or make the person conscious of mortal sin? Since laws are quicker to release than to bind,[367] it is better to give an account of God as having too much mercy rather than too much severity, as Chrysostom[368] says....So it is better that absolution be given.[369]

Gabriel Biel, who lived about the year 1480, wrote in the same way: "Nothing should be condemned as a mortal sin about which there is not a clear argument or the manifest authority of Scripture."[370]

Saint Thomas teaches the same: "The person, therefore, who gives assent to the opinion of some master or other, against the clear witness of Scripture or against what is publicly held according to the authority of the Church, cannot be excused from the fault of error."[371] Therefore, St. Thomas only condemns the person who follows an opinion against the clear witness of Scripture, or against the common judgment of the authority of the Church. He does not condemn a person who follows an opinion which is not opposed to certain law, as John Nider notes:

> These words of St. Thomas cannot be understood except of those things that are clearly evident from Scripture or by a decision of the Church, as being against the law of God. It is not to be understood of those things where the above is not clear, as commented on in the third appendix to *Quodlibet* article 10: saying otherwise would contradict myself in the same book.[372]

Saint Thomas gives the same teaching elsewhere:

> Every question, in which there is an inquiry about mortal sin, is most hazardous to determine, unless the truth of the matter has been expressly clarified. This is because error, by which something is believed not to be a mortal sin when it is a mortal sin, does not excuse conscience in everything, even though it excuses from a lot. A true error, by which it is believed to be a mortal sin, binds in conscience as mortal sin.[373]

Note the words: *unless the truth is expressly available, it is most hazardous to determine it.* Therefore, the principle of our adversaries is a false one that in doubt the law is in possession and, accordingly, the safer position is to be taken when in doubt.

Fr. Patuzzi continues: if liberty is in possession, why does St. Thomas write that, in doubt, following the more benign view *does not excuse from everything*? It is to be answered that the holy doctor is here not talking about the final practical judgment, which could become certain on the basis of a certain reflex principle. He is talking only of the direct judgment, which is doubtful, since both opinions are doubtful. Thus, he says that the person is not excused who, only from a direct judgment, embraces the more benign view. It would however be otherwise, says St. Antoninus, if something is taken from a probable opinion. Understand this (as) the ultimate certain practical dictate that is derived from a certain reflex principle. Let us listen to the holy archbishop:

> To be noted is what St. Thomas said in that question in the *Quodlibetales,* namely the question in which it is inquired whether a certain act be a mortal sin or not. Unless there is available [in reference to it] the express authority of sacred Scripture, or the canons, or a decision of the Church, or clear reason, it would be most dangerous to determine it as mortal sin. For if it is determined that there is a mortal sin, and there is not, the person would sin mortally by going against the law, because everything that is against conscience builds [the road] to hell...but if it is determined that it is not a mortal sin, and according to the truth of the matter it is [a mortal sin], the person's error would not excuse one from mortal sin. This second view seems reasonably understandable, when evidently one could be making the error from crass ignorance: otherwise it is only from a probable opinion.

The archbishop continues:

Think of an example: when someone consulted experts on a certain issue and they say to him that such a matter is not a mortal sin: you can see, then, that there is almost invincible ignorance in this person, which excuses him from everything. This applies also to those things that are not expressly against divine law, or the natural law, or against the articles of faith, the Ten Commandments and the like: in such matters the person who does not know will be overlooked...if it is said that here is [a case of] usury, and that usury is not against the Decalogue, it is to be answered: to say that usury is against the precepts of the Decalogue is truly a banal statement; but in this case it is not clear that the contract is one of usury, since learned people give opposing views against each other on the issue.[374]

Thus, according to St. Thomas and St. Antoninus, where the truth is not patently obvious, the law, being doubtful, does not oblige.

ARTICLE 76
A third objection and answer

Our opponent makes a third objection: nothing is allowed to us except what is in conformity to the divine will. I am delighted that he makes this objection, because on this point St. Thomas teaches all that is sufficient to completely endorse my position. The angelic doctor asks: "In order to be good, must an act of the human will be conformed to the divine will as to the object willed?"[375] He says that people are bound to conform to the divine will in matters of the *formal* will, namely *regarding the will for the common good*. A person could not lawfully will something except what is good. They are not so bound, however, in matters of the *material* will. Then the holy doctor objects to himself:

> It seems that the human will ought not always be con-
> formed to the divine will as to the object it wills. For we
> cannot will what we do not know, since the will's objec-
> tive is a good thing that is apprehended. Yet we do not
> know in most cases what God wills for us. Hence, our will
> cannot be conformed to the divine will as to the object
> willed.[376]

Moreover, he answers:

> As to what God wills for us, we may know in some way as
> to its general nature, for we know that whatever God wills
> he wills because it is truly good. Hence, whoever wills a
> thing because of any real quality of goodness has a will
> conformed to the divine will with regard to the reason for
> willing it, which is the formal or common will.[377]

He then adds: "Nevertheless, we may not know what God wills for us in a particular case and in this sense we are not bound to conform our will to his."[378] Therefore, a person is not bound to conform himself to the divine will in specifics, even in respect of the divine precepts, where the will of God has not yet made this manifest to a person. Fr. Gonet says very clearly: "A person is not bound to be conformed to the divine will in the material will, except when the divine will is made known to us by a precept or a prohibition."[379] Fr. Patuzzi insists:

With regard to a precept and prohibition [it is better to make note of this in his own words] we ought always conform ourselves to the divine will, also as regards the material will. God has given us his precepts so that we may observe them, and these are already sufficiently notified in his laws.[380]

However, I ask: If a precept is doubtful and obscure, as can happen in the conflict between two equally probable opinions, how can it be said that a precept has been made sufficiently known? Then, it is not a precept that has been given sufficient notification, but only a doubt about a precept. This is exactly as we indicated above; when two equally probable opinions are in competition with each other, neither is probable and only doubt remains. As a result, in that case it can only be said that we have a doubt about a precept, but not knowledge of it. Honestly, how could we ever say that we have knowledge of the law when strictly we don't know if the law exists or not? Then it is better that we say that we do not know the law, and so we are not bound by it. This is in line with what St. Thomas says about being conformed to the divine will in questions of the material will. God does not order us to obey his will when that has not yet been made known to us.

With respect to our case, St. Thomas confirms this most expressly in another place,[381] where the question is: *whether God is to be obeyed in all matters.* He responds affirmatively. However, later he argues to himself in the third objection:

Anyone who obeys God matches his will to God's even in regard to the matter willed. We are not bound in all cases, however, to conform to the divine will as to what we will as I have already pointed out. We do not have to give obedience to God, therefore, in every case.[382]

Here is how he responds: "Granted that a person is not always bound to will the same thing God wills, he is bound to will what God wants him to will. Moreover, the knowledge of what this is comes chiefly through the divine commandments."[383] However, how do we know what it is that God wills for us? We know, according to St. Thomas, when it is *principally known through a divine precept*. Doubtful knowledge of the precept does not therefore suffice for us to be bound to observe a precept as the will of God. It is required, over and above, that we have certain and manifest notification of the precept. This indeed is the meaning of the word *becomes known*.[384]

I ask a question and conclude this point. In the case where the divine will as regards the observance of particular precepts is not yet made known to us, are we bound to conform to it? Not at all, the angelic doctor says: but, if *in a particular instance we do not know what God wills, we are not bound to conform our will to the divine will in this matter*. Fr. Gonet clearly confirms this, as we saw: "A person is not bound to be conformed to the divine will at the level of the material will, except when the divine will is made manifest to us as a precept or a prohibition."[385] Indeed, John Gerson writes, as we recorded elsewhere, that not even God obliges his creatures to observe his will unless he has, in a prior moment, made it known to them. "It is necessary to make known the ordinance and will of God since, by his will alone, God is unable, as yet, to absolutely impose obligations on a human creature."[386]

From this it is clear, and a point on which St. Thomas was always constant in his teaching, that laws have to be certain in order to oblige. In all the places where he speaks about the matter, he always makes use of precise words that clearly show what was his thinking on the matter. He says that law, in order to be obligatory, must be made known to us in order to be applicable. He says that promulgation of the law occurs "from this fact that

God puts it into the minds of humans so that it might be naturally known."[387] He says be naturally known. Therefore, a person is obliged to observe the law when the person knows the law, and not when he has doubts about the law. He says that law is the measure by which a person ought to be measured. Thus, he says that "this measure ought to be most certain."[388] He writes that just as a rope does not bind unless it is applied to the thing to be bound through contact with it, so a precept does not bind except through knowledge of it. He adds: "Whence no one is bound by any precept, except through the knowledge of that precept."[389] He states that a person is therefore only bound to obey God when the divine will is primarily made known through divine precepts.[390] Thus, according to all these doctrines of St. Thomas, it is to be concluded that the divine law does not oblige unless it is *known* and *most certainly so;* and that it is proper *knowledge* that has been *made manifest.*

For this reason, having demonstrated all this, the objection of our opponent is wide of the mark; opinions being equally probable, the safer opinion, even if it does not lead to a certain obligation, at least leads to a probable obligation. As a result, a morally certain dictate about the goodness of an action would be lacking and, without that, it is not lawful to act. I have answered this objection many times above, specifically: when two equally probable opinions are in competition with each other, the opinion in favor of the law does not give rise to an obligation unless the doubt has been removed. A doubt of this type, according to the opinion of all the probabilists and the probabiliorists, even of Fr. Patuzzi himself, could be properly disposed of, not only from a direct principle, but even from a definite reflex principle, through which certainty about the goodness of the action is thus established.

ARTICLE 77
A fourth objection and answer

Patuzzi makes a fourth objection. There is a rule from the sacred canons: "In matters of doubt, the safer way is to be chosen" as found in the chapter *Illud Dominus de clerico excom. deposito.* The same is repeated in the chapter *Ad audientiam, de hominic* and in the chapter *Petitio tua, eod. tit.* It is also found in the *Exivi* of Clement (at the words *Item quia*) and in the chapter *Juvenis, de sponsal.* Our opponent says that these canons speak in a general way about all doubts. Therefore, broadly speaking, they are to be accepted. I respond and concede that, usually speaking, they are to be accepted as regards all practical doubts and doubts of fact such as those that occur in respect of the abovementioned canons. However, they are not applicable to speculative doubts and doubts of law, as affirmed by St. Antoninus, Christianus Lupus, John Nider, Dominic Soto, Suarez, Tabiana, Silvester, Angelus, Henriques, Angles, St. Bonaventure, Gerson, Pelbart, and almost all the others in general, as we shall soon see. They say that the abovementioned rule of the canons, insofar as it concerns speculative doubts, is a counsel and not a precept. Look at the way St. Antoninus writes:

> Some introduce the saying "in matters of doubt the safer way is to be chosen." It is to be answered: this is true about the goodness and the greatness of the merit, but not about the necessity of salvation as regards all doubts. Otherwise, it would be necessary for everyone to enter consecrated life.[391]

The words of St. Antoninus are very clear. However, Fr. Patuzzi says that the holy archbishop is speaking only of that which is the more benevolent view as the only true one.[392] He assumes from the words "otherwise it would be necessary for all to enter consecrated life." Therefore, Fr. Patuzzi claims, St. Antoninus wishes to speak here of two opinions that are equally safe and morally certain. He attempts to prove that St. Antoninus writes, by force of the rule mentioned, that in all opinions that are doubtful the safer one is to be chosen.

Let us clarify the issue, granting that this is what St. Antoninus puts forward when he is speaking of a type of contract about which there is a heated discussion among learned people. It is disputed whether a particular contract is one of usury or not. The saint writes:

> It is said that this is usury, and usury is against the Decalogue. It is answered that usury is against the precepts of the Decalogue, and this is indeed true in an indirect sense. However, whether this contract is one of usury is not clear, since learned scholars offer opposing views among themselves on the matter. When it is said that ignorance of the natural law is not an excuse, this is to be understood in the sense of those things that expressly, by themselves or indirectly, are against natural or divine law, as being against faith and the commandments, for clear reasons or by a decision of the Church or…the common view of doctors. It is not true of those matters—many, mediate, unclear—that are not clearly proven as precepts and articles of faith.[393]

He then adds:

> Those wishing to prove that a contract is illicit introduce the principle "in matters of doubt the safer way is to be cho-

sen." It is to be answered that this is true about the goodness and greatness of the merit but not about the necessity of salvation as regards all doubts: otherwise it would be necessary for all people to enter consecrated life.[394]

In no way, therefore, did St. Antoninus think that there is a universal law which states that the safer views are to be followed in all doubts. In speculative doubts, when two opinions are in competition with each other, as in the case being discussed, he gives his opinion that the quoted rule of the canons is not at the level of a precept. It is not...forbidden, in the example mentioned, even if it is absurd, that in some cases it might be opportune that one enters the consecrated life. The saint is not speaking here against those who would presume that all are bound by a precept, that they enter the consecrated life. However, he answers directly to those who would say that the contract is forbidden on the basis of the rule obliging everyone to follow the safer path.

Let us repeat the words already given above: Those wishing to prove that the contract is illicit introduce this argument: *in matters of doubt the safer way is to be chosen.* This phrase is, however, precisely about a contract at the level of a speculative doubt. Saint Antoninus answers: *This is true about goodness and the importance of merit, but not as regards the necessity of salvation in respect of all doubts.* Hence, it is not correct to say that St. Antoninus wishes to talk about a person who initiates a contract with what he judges to be, not doubtful, but definitely lawful.

The holy archbishop does not wish only to speak of an opinion that may be true for this one case, but about a contract that was unlawful because the canons prescribed that in matters of doubt the safer way is to be followed. Otherwise, against the objection of those who wished to prove that the safer way be chosen, it would be useless to reply that it *is about goodness and the greatness of merit, not about necessity as regards all doubts.* It should be answered that one follows the rule only in doubt, but not when the person acting has formed as true his own opinion. The saint says that the rule of the canons is not that of a universal precept *as regards all doubt.* He is speaking only *about goodness and the greatness of merit.*

Of the same view as St. Antoninus are the following. John Nider: "To follow the safer way is a matter of counsel, not of precept."[395] Tabiena: "It is not true that in matters of doubt the safer way is to be chosen, because this is not a precept but a counsel."[396] See Navarrus,[397] Dominic Soto, Abbas, Silvester,[398] Suarez,[399] Angles,[400] Henriques.[401] Confer also St. Bonaventure and Gerson, etc., as cited in Terillus.[402]

ARTICLE 78
Further responses

With regard to the cases related in the canons, it is absolutely necessary to follow the rule, because the doubts were practical and doubts of fact. There could not be any certain principle, direct or reflex, by which the obligation of following the safer path could be excused, because of the scandals and other evils, which ought to be avoided in these cases. In order that this might be clearly explained, it is appropriate to briefly discuss here what touches upon the cases and decisions in the text of those who object to us. In the chapter *Illud Dominus, de clerico excommun. deposito etc.,* the case was about a particular bishop who, notwithstanding the public notoriety of the excommunication brought against him, was not afraid to celebrate. For this reason, we say that he had been disciplined in the statement of Innocent III. When the doubt about the excommunication persisted, he would have been bound to show due diligence so that he would become more certain of the truth. Meanwhile he ought to have abstained from celebrating. In this regard, quite correctly the Pope said *because in doubt it is better that the safer way be chosen, even if there were a doubt about the sentence imposed on him, he ought to have refrained rather than be involved with ecclesiastical sacraments.*

As regards the chapter *Ad audientiam, de homicidio voluntario,* the case is about a particular priest who inflicted a wound on a man, from which the man died. Later, it was doubted whether the man had died as a result of this wound. Clement III decreed that it would be more appropriate that the priest discontinue the celebration of the sacrifice of the Mass. This is what he said: *Since in doubtful things one ought to choose the safer way, it is appropriate for you to order the priest that he does not act as a minister in sacred orders.* Here, at this point, it should be noted that the truth of the fact had not been fully explored, so that it would be beyond doubt that the death of the person had occurred as a result of the wound. Hence, the text adds: *if truly the person had died from another illness...he could celebrate the divine offices.* The Pope wisely decreed that in the meantime the priest should not celebrate: he said that, in a doubt of this type, the safer way is to be chosen. It should be noted, secondly, with Navarrus and Suarez, that one is not dealing with a precept that ought to be observed, but only with something that is considered appropriate. If it were afterward established that the priest was a murderer, it would have been perceived as a scandal by the people to have seen him celebrate. A similar point was established in a comparable case of doubtful homicide in the chapter *Petitio tua, 24, de homicidio voluntario.* This states that *it is more prudent in doubts of this kind to desist from rather than venture to celebrate.* Who cannot see that it is necessary in such cases, in order to avoid scandal, that it is more appropriate that the safer way be chosen, that is, not to celebrate?

To the *Exivi* of Clement we answer that, in this case, the Friars Minor had urgently requested the Apostolic See whether they were absolutely bound *sub gravi* by those rules of religion that were drawn up in the language of a precept. The Pope responded: *in those things which regard the welfare of the soul, in order to avoid severe torments of conscience, the safer position is to be taken.* In the first place, as Fr. Eusebius Amort thinks, when the Pope says *the safer position is to be taken,* he does not mean it to be understood as speaking of material security in choosing the safer part. He is thinking of the formal security of conscience by acting with moral certainty and without practical doubt. If, in fact, the Pope meant material security, he would surely have said that all opinions in the imperative mode denote a precept and that materially the safer way is removed from doubt.

However, the Pope says that only those words are to be taken as imperatives which are clear *from the force of the words,* or by the idiom of the words, or *at least by reason of the matter in question.* Moreover, he asks:

> The Friars may not be bound to the observance of all those things which are inserted in the rule using the imperative mode, as they would be bound to the observance of the commandments or precepts of equal weight. However, it is expedient for the Friars themselves to observe the purity of the rule and maintain its rigor in respect of those things that are of the same weight as precepts. If they come to know of them, they are obliged to follow them, as will be noted below.

After this, the Pope mentions those things that are to be regarded as precepts. This is how Fr. Eusebius Amort responds to the letter of Pope Clement:[403]

I give another, and more conclusive, answer. The case was the one as we read in that text. Earlier it was doubted by the Friars whether the rule bound them only with regard to the vows of poverty, chastity, and obedience. Pope Nicholas II stated that it was binding also with regard to the evangelical counsels that were expressed in the rule with the obligatory words of a precept or of an instruction of equal weight. The Friars then petitioned Clement V to give an answer about *what...are they to consider as precepts of equal weight*? Before he explained that those things which seemed to be of the same weight as precepts by the form of the words and by reason of the grave matter that was at stake, Clement premised his remarks with these words: *to avoid grave remorse of conscience* the safer part is to be chosen. Consequently, in that case, it is not a question of two equally probable parts.

The question is whether the obligation remained of following that part which, according to the rigor of the rule and according to what Nicholas III had already declared, that it was not only safer to do this but that it was the only safe way. Since it was already stated, by the force of the words and the gravity of the matter, that one was obliged to follow as precepts not only the three principal vows of religious life, but also the evangelical counsels contained in the rule, they could not be overlooked without grave remorse of conscience. For this reason, Clement said, to avoid remorse of this kind, the safer way is to be followed that, in fact, was the only way that was true and secure. On the other side, no reasons are sufficient which would have the weight of excusing the infringement of those counsels from being a grave fault.

Finally, from the chapter *Juvenis 3 de sponsal* there is the case of a youth of seven years of age who took a young girl as his bride and, on her death, afterward contracted a new wedding with a cousin of hers. From this, a doubt arose about the validity of the first wedding on account of the impotency of a seven-year-old. Eugenius III instructed that the young man should be separated from the cousin, for the sake of the good name of the Church. He added: *because, therefore, in those matters which we deem doubtful, we are bound to hold that which we deem to be more certain.*

Having said all this, we maintain that (a) the Pope ordered the separation in law, not because he thought that in doubtful opinions the safer way is to be followed, but because the separation was necessary to avoid scandal, and to keep the good name of the Church properly secured. We state (b) that the Pope, preferring the words *that which we deem more certain, we are bound to follow* did not say this with regard to the youth who, anyhow, was properly aware at the time of the first marriage whether he was potent or impotent, but in respect of the judge who, in the court, had to decide when the arguments on the different sides are doubtful. In this case, it is beyond doubt that we are bound to follow what is more certain. Hence, he says *more certain* (not safer) since the Pope judged it as more certain that a separation should be imposed because the doubt still persisted about the validity of the first marriage. It is marriage that has stronger claims. There is a difference between this and our question, where it is a question in the internal forum, and not about a doubt of fact or of an opinion that is equally probable. From this it is clear that all doubts pertinent to the text of the case were practical doubts and doubts of fact which in no way can be solved by a reflex principle.

This is obviously the correct view because the Popes themselves, in speculative doubts, did not always use the rule that the safer way is to be followed. Adrian VI, as Dominic Soto recalls, despite the fact he personally held the opposite view, gave a dispensation in some ratified marriage: he relies simply on the judgment of Cajetan. Besides, in the chapter *Laudabiliem, de frigiditate* there is the case that the Pope conceded to a couple, who were doubtful of their power to copulate, that they attempt marriage for a three-year period. If a doubtful law is always to be observed, as our adversary wishes, and the doubt is whether the woman was actually opposed to having intercourse, how could the Pope allow the man access to her for a three-year period to attempt copulation?

Consider another point. If that law had been universal, it would have to be followed in all doubts, even speculative ones. The safer view must always be chosen, so that not even a more probable opinion could be held. In any case, this opinion was not safer but remained within the bounds of probability. This view cannot be held, since it was proscribed in the proposition of Alexander VII. *It is not lawful to follow an opinion, which among the probable opinions is the most probable.* Add also that, even if the matter were doubtful, the above mentioned rule of the canons would be understood about all doubts, and not only about practical doubts. The reasons which show that a doubtful law is not sufficiently proven, as it has not been adequately promulgated, are the same reasons which prove that this decree from the canons is not a universal law as regards all doubts but only regarding doubts of fact and practical doubts.

Finally, so that we can bring the present discussion to an end, I ask: What do the canons teach? (I will not be giving any attention to what might be said in response to my reasoning.) They lay down that in doubts the safer way is to be chosen. It is said: *in doubts.* What if we are not in doubt? What prevents that law from being applied if a person bases his opinion on a definite principle? Thus, he already forms for himself a morally certain conscience about the goodness of an action, and he finds a way out from the boundaries of doubt. It can be no longer said that the person is in doubt. Even our adversary concedes that the previously mentioned rule of following the safer rule has no place in matters of justice. But if the rule of the canons is that what is safer is to be followed, in a universal way for all doubts, even for a person who legitimately owns something, and is in doubt whether the thing belongs to another, and he fears that it could be taken from him, goes against what St. Augustine says: "In manor law, as long as someone can be correctly said to be a possessor in good faith, during that time he can ignore whether another is the owner."[404]

ARTICLE 79
A fifth objection and answers

There is a fifth objection. A decision of an assembly of French bishops decreed that in a question of equally probable opinions, the safer one was to be chosen. I have the greatest respect for the authority of these prelates, but everyone teaches that the extrinsic authority of learned people cannot be of pivotal weight where the intrinsic reasoning seems certain and convincing. This is all the more so when the intrinsic reasoning is itself not lacking in sufficient authority from others. I, however, draw attention to the fact that, for our judgment, there is not less extrinsic authority than for the opposite view; the fact is that it is much greater. Nor can it be denied that our judgment, for about eighty or even ninety years, was the common view among authors of the moral science, among whom were very many cardinals, bishops, doctors of the universities, and notably, many masters of the Dominican Order, among whom a high level of learning always flourished. Here, for the sake of brevity, I omit their names and the citation of their propositions, which I have already given in my little work that was published under separate cover with the title: *On the moderate use of the probable opinion.*[405]

Nor is it worth stating that the authority of these people in this matter is to be given little value, even by me. My opponents have treated me as the one being misled, though they based themselves on the principle that I myself rejected: *the person who acts with probability, acts with prudence.* I have already stated at the beginning of this dissertation that such a principle, on its own, and taken as *per se* assumed, is not sufficient to justify proper use of the equally probable opinion. However, I draw attention to the fact that already many authors (as we saw above), in order to uphold our judgment, based their stand on our other principle, namely that a doubtful law does not apply. Besides, I say that those authors did not only use that principle *the person who acts with probability, etc.* In this way I bring the issues together.

On the one side these authors already acknowledge that, to act lawfully, it is necessary to have moral certainty about the goodness of an action. Against this, indeed, the same authors repeat in various places our other principles, namely, that a law that is not sufficiently promulgated does not oblige, and that where liberty is in possession, an uncertain law cannot impose a definite obligation. From that principle, now approved by these authors, they say that *in doubt the condition of the person in possession is better.* Therefore, by using principles of this kind, speaking of the use of probable opinions, at least they undoubtedly presuppose it even if they do not expressly mention it. Hence, it is correctly thought that those who use the phrase *the person who acts with probability, acts with prudence* employ it as a sort of corollary or a consequence that can be inferred from reflex principles. This is all the more so because the topic of the probable opinion was at that time very confused; discussion about it was baffling, and as a result the older authors talked about it in a more muddled way.

Moreover, the phrase *the person who acts with probability, etc.* can be understood in a double sense. If it is accepted as being based on other reflex principles, it is truly certain and prudent; if however it is accepted as a direct principle, with the consideration of judgment discounted, it is false. Hence, regarding that dictum, taken in a direct sense, the prelates of France correctly did not hesitate. They consider the phrase within a context: *In doubts about a question of health, where equal weights of reasons are offered to the mind on both sides, we should follow that which is safer, or in a particular case the one that is alone safe. Here we are dealing with precepts and not with counsels, as Scripture says: he who loves danger will die in that danger.* Giving close attention to these latter words, it appears as definite that the prelates themselves were speaking of a person acting with a practical doubt and who did not have a principle by which the doubt could be eliminated. However, if they preferred to speak of a person forming a definitive judgment, not from probability alone, but from another certain reflex principle, I think that the prelates would have described the matter differently.

I am writing about the many edicts of bishops, issued from France. Fr. Patuzzi transcribes them in his work *La Regola Prossima delle Umane Azioni* and he credits them in a postscript as forbidding the probable opinion. I read those things carefully, and I considered all of them to precisely reflect a book with the title *Apologia Casistarum* that was quite correctly condemned. It asserts that overly lax principles can never be held as secure. An opinion (and not only the less probable but also the more probably probable) could be followed on the basis of the authority of four or three authors, indeed even of one only. For that reason, the above-cited edict is not, or only minimally, opposed to our view.

For the rest, the weight of intrinsic reason should be given the principal attention because extrinsic authority does not have any other effect than to reinforce and strengthen the presumption of the intrinsic reason. I consider that it is already convincing and evident. Many others share this view with me. As regards the extrinsic authority of the doctors, I believe that I have shown this in a most sufficient way, as demonstrated above. This is all the more so, since we can observe that our adversary did not respond to our arguments in any adequate way. On the other side, even if the arguments had value, they would only prove the most carefully condemned view is certain.

Speaking of those who, while not writing specifically in favor of the rigid system, but only approve of it orally, I have respect for them all and consider them wiser than I am. However, I say that these would carry greater authority with me if I knew that they had considered, in a mature way, the reasons for both opinions. I greatly doubt this, and with good reason. I note that authors of a rigid view, and which are approved by these people, either give negligible attention to our arguments, or respond to them with equivocations and lies, to which any intelligent person could very easily respond. I add that supporters of this way of thinking, in general (as I mentioned above), reflect on direct motives but they apply their mind, either very little or not at all, to take note of reflex principles. For that matter, these demand much deliberation. I hold it as certain that reflection of this type is given minimal attention by those people who today show themselves off and play on the fact that they are antiprobabilists. Let us move on, because the material is unpleasant and I have little appetite to explain myself further on it. In the booklet about this controversy that I published very recently, I give in the notes many opinions of bishops, abbots, and other learned people in which they do not doubt to call our *system* true and certain.

ARTICLE 80
Another objection and a response

My opponent raises a sixth objection using the text of Ecclesiasticus 3:27, "He who loves danger will die in that danger." Therefore, he says, the person who puts himself in danger of transgressing the law, already sins. However, it is to be noted here how an equivocation or an ambiguity emerges. The person who uses an equally probable opinion, basing himself on a definite principle, is one who is in danger of transgressing the law, but not of sinning. Why so? In what way does the person not sin who exposes himself to the danger of transgressing the law? I repeat: he does not sin. It is necessary, therefore, to distinguish a certain law from an uncertain one.

When the law is certain, undoubtedly we cannot expose ourselves to the danger of transgressing. It is like the danger of delaying our own conversion until the point of death, as stated in the text quoted: *he will have a hardened heart at the end, and he who loves danger will die in it.* The law of charity is certain: everyone should have respect for themselves and not continue any longer in sin, on account of the danger of dying in sin. In that way, loving this danger, he will die in it. Our adversary similarly objects to the doctrine of St. Thomas, which coincides with this: "Whoever commits himself to the danger...of mortal sin, sins mortally."[406]

These words can be explained in two ways: either of putting oneself in the danger of transgressing a certain law, as conveyed in the case taken from Scripture, or of the person acting with a practical doubt, in line with the other text of the holy doctor: "The person who does something or omits to do it, in which he doubts whether there be mortal sin, sins mortally by putting himself in the danger."[407] Please take note: the angelic doctor does not say "in which there is a danger of breaking the law," but in which there *is a doubt whether there be a mortal sin.* Elsewhere the same St. Thomas speaking of an uncertain precept, says: "No one is bound by a precept...except through the knowledge of that precept."[408]

ARTICLE 81
Further clarification

Our opponent says that, when the law is doubtful, the person who puts himself in danger of transgressing the law, certainly sins. He relies on the text from Scripture: *the one who loves danger will die in the danger.* I take up the topic one more time, namely, that to avoid danger, it is always necessary to take the strictest view. One ought never act other than with absolute moral certitude and free from every fear that the opinion which one has chosen to follow is true. In no way, he responds, is it enough that the opinion be most probable. The opposite proposition was already proscribed by Alexander VIII: *It is not licit to follow an opinion, even the most probable among the probable opinions.* In the first place, therefore, I assert the following. It is not a correct conclusion to deduce that, the law being certain, a person who exposes himself to the danger of transgressing the law actually sins. Even in working with the most probable opinion, the person encounters the danger (however remote) of breaking the law.

I wish to add something (and on this point I will dwell a little). A person can believe that it is never lawful to endanger oneself by transgressing the law, and against that asserts that it is possible to hold the less safe view, but only when it is a most probable one. It is with great difficulty, and hardly ever, that one could be persuaded to follow this view with a safe conscience, unless the person finds it to be certain in the strict sense and leaves him protected from all fear. Here is the reasoning: The most probable opinion is that which, even if it has the highest grade of probability, does not however exceed the bounds of probability. This is in accord with the terms of the proposition reported above condemning *the most probable among the probable opinions.* Thus, as the doctors commonly affirm, the most probable opinion, which could even be called morally certain (speaking, however, in a broad manner) does not exclude all prudent fear. Here is the difference with the opinion or judgment that is strictly certain by excluding all prudent fear.

If, therefore, the most probable opinion does not exclude all prudent fear, the opposite opinion of the probabilists is not capable of doing so, either. Such an opinion is only vaguely probable, and vague probability is not probability at all. It merely has a deceptive appearance or a hollow understanding of probability; it is not capable of producing a prudent sense of fear but only some thoughtless sense of terror. Imprudent fear is not a proper fear that would have the value of taking away any danger of sin. Even the very rigid and strict tutiorists commonly say that ill-considered fears of this type are to be regarded as negligible. There is no justification for them.

It is foolish to suggest that God would impose futile and irrational fears that had to be avoided. Thus, strictly speaking, the opinion of the probabilists is not that they are against that which is questionable but that they oppose what is doubtfully probable. The most probable opinions, as we have said, are not lacking all prudent fear that may be false. The opposite opinion of the probabilists is not lacking in every prudent motive, which may be true.

I accept that there is a concern when the opinion in favor of the law is opposed by the opinion of the probabilists in favor of liberty and so is doubtfully probable. How can those who think it is unlawful to place oneself in danger of transgressing the law, wishing to follow the more probable opinion, be able in practice and with a tranquil conscience to act with conviction? One can use the most probable opinion; otherwise, one would be exposed to the danger of transgressing the law. Where will you find a weighing scale so exact and so safe that the opinion in favor of the law would lack the weight of probability to make it probable, so that a person could securely proceed and act free from danger? On this I repeat what I said at the beginning. The person who is not capable of holding in practice some less safe opinion, unless it is the most probable, will have great difficulty being able to form a precept of conscience that is certain enough to act on. This will be the case unless he holds to the strictly most safe view that alone could free him and leave him protected from any danger of transgressing the law.

ARTICLE 82
It is mistaken to make the law overly rigid

Our opponent persists by saying: the person who holds the safer opinions will advance more safely. Here is my reply: It is indeed unjust to relax the observance of divine laws more than is allowed, but it is not less wrong to make the divine burden heavier for others than it ought to be. Too much severity (writes Cabassutius):

> While it pushes people to higher things…it also obstructs the way of eternal salvation. It condemns the saved (as St. Bonaventure says) by making them aware of their own weakness and so adds to their sense of desperation. It happens as a result that, feeling themselves to be miserable human creatures, they believe or doubt that they are in mortal guilt where there is none…however, on account of being overcome with the difficulty of the matter, be-

cause of their erroneous conscience, they do sin mortally and are damned.[409]

Saint Bonaventure aptly writes:

A too-loose conscience is to be avoided as well as a too-strict one, since the former generates presumption and the latter despair. The first type of conscience often says that the bad is good and the second type, on the other hand, says that the good is bad. The first view often saves the damned and the second, on the contrary, damns those who are saved.[410]

On this point, John Gerson shrewdly writes:

Doctors of theology should not be too facile in asserting that some things are mortal sins, where they are not most certain of the matter. By those type of rigid and excessively strict assertions in general matters, people are unable to rise from the quagmire of being sinners. They fall more deeply into it because, being desperate, they become immersed by it. What does it benefit, indeed what obstacle does it not create, to force the commandment of God more than is needed? God's law is indeed very broad.[411]

Very wisely, St. Chrysostom instructs us: "Regarding your own life be severe, regarding others be benign."[412] Fr. Suarez adds: "The greatest danger for souls is incurred if we impose too many restrictions on them in doubtful cases."[413] Cardinal Pallavicinus explains the same thing more extensively:

As regards yourself, that assertion "in doubt the safer part is to be chosen" is most true, if correctly understood. It is true whether we are dealing with a practical choice because here we should always follow the safest one because it ought to be evidently lawful...or whether it is about the choice of a speculative opinion. As regards the choice in this judgment, what gives the greater security should be sought. However, the greater security in a judgment is not the greater security in an action...the opinion is proposed that we are always held to do what is more secure in action, even if it involves a material transgression. This opinion is not only not safer, but ignoring it involves the greatest exposure to the danger of formal transgression, which is the opposite of acting in a safe way.[414]

The Dominican Fr. Bancel writes in a similar manner:

Many are the things which it is safer to do: but, at the same time, it is also safer not to believe that we are obliged to do them...unless it is obvious that you are morally certain of the obligation.[415]

From this, the same author concludes:

Since we are not obliged to form our conscience about an obligation to do something under pain of sin, unless it is morally agreed that there is such an obligation, we ought not to impose that burden on ourselves. When, on the other hand, we are morally certain of exemption from such an obligation, it is morally clear to us that our liberty has a greater sway in choosing whichever of the opinions we wish to.[416]

To be completely truthful, when I began to occupy myself with the science of moral theology, and because it happened when I was studying under a master of the rigid opinion, I too strove hugely for this view against others at that particular time. Later, after better discussing the arguments of this controversy, the opposite view, which is in favor of the equally probable opinion, seemed to me to be morally certain. I became convinced that I should adopt the principle that has been repeated here many times: a doubtful law cannot oblige. From this time, I became convinced that it is harmful to conscience, when opinions are equally probable, to be obliged to follow the safer opinion, with the danger of being led into many formal sins.

However, since I began to notice sharp attacks being made in this controversy against the milder opinion, many times I diligently went over this point to find a more balanced expression. Reading and rereading all the authors, as many as I could put my hands on among the moderns who argued in favor of the more rigid view, I was ready to abandon my view as soon as it no longer appeared certain to me. As a result, there are many opinions, which once I considered probable, that I was not ashamed of rejecting later on. Thus, and indeed all the more so, I would not have been ashamed of retracting a view that concerned a matter of greater importance.

The more diligently I was anxious to assess the arguments for our opinions, all the more certain did they appear to me. For the rest, if there is anyone who can enlighten me with stronger reasons about the falsity of the two principles that I have taken care to express here, I would be most grateful. Indeed, I would promise to make my revocation in public. Until, however, I feel otherwise than I do at the present moment, and until I have not been persuaded otherwise, I say, without serious regret of conscience, that I could not bind others to follow the safer view, when the opinions are equally probable, unless the Church declares otherwise. If it so declares, I willingly submit my judgment to it.

I assert that I do not approve of those confessors who, adhering to too great an austerity, easily condemn the use of many opinions that lack a serious foundation. Equally so, on the opposite side, I cannot approve of those confessors who use facile opinions without a definite foundation as if they could be called probable opinions. The confessor, before he holds any opinion, is always bound to weigh up the intrinsic arguments. When some reason occurs to him that is convincing for the safer view, then he cannot follow the opposite less safe view, even though the authority of many doctors might favor it. In this way it is not authority that is of the major weight, as compared to the weight to be given to a reasoned argument, according to what St. Thomas teaches: "A person with scant learning is surer of something he hears from an expert than he is of any insight of his own."[417] However, a case of this type is indeed very rare.

ARTICLE 83
When to use the benign or the strict opinion

So much for the theory. Insofar as it touches on the practice of choosing opinions, it is common to ask: *Is it appropriate to prefer the rigid or the benign opinion?* Here is my answer: When it is a question of removing a penitent from the danger of formal sin, the confessor, generally speaking and in so far as Christian prudence suggests, should use the benign opinion. Where, in truth, the benign opinions bring back the danger of formal sin, as is the opinion of quite a number of authors, for example regarding avoiding the proximate occasions of sin and the like, then it is always more expedient that the confessor is bound to use the safer opinions.

This will help the penitents to keep themselves in the state of grace. I say this because the confessor is the doctor of souls.

I do not know in what way it can be taught with a good conscience (generally speaking) that penitents who, on the basis of completing the confession of their guilt, and had at that moment an evident right to absolution, can be now denied it, simply because the penitent caught between two opinions of equal weight, does not wish to follow the safer one. This is the type of rigidity that I consider without any doubt to be immoderate and unjust. This type of austerity could be the cause of many souls being damned. I find there are many other authors, even among the probabiliorists, modern ones as well as earlier ones, mentioned indeed by their adversaries as defenders of the rigid opinion, who in fact teach the opposite view. Listen to what the probabiliorist Pontas says:

> It is to be recognized, however, that if the confessor were persuaded that the opinion of his penitent…was probable [one is speaking of an opinion to which the opposite opinion is safer] then he can give absolution, provided however…that he does not act against his own conscience.[418]

If the confessor can absolve the penitent, this is because the penitent has the right to absolution. The probabiliorist Cabassutius writes in a similar way:

> Any confessor ought to absolve a penitent who does not wish to abstain from his action, since, according to the probable opinion of spiritual people and doctors and some others not condemned by the Church authority, it is lawful to do so. This is true although, according to the equally probable opinion of other authorities, that the

confessor himself follows, it is held to be less probable [to be understood as not notably less so]…as Navarrus…Silvius….and others demonstrate.[419]

He explains the reason for this:

Since the confessor acts with regard to the other person and not according to his own personal opinion, but not however against his own personal conscience, he ought to judge that this person here and now is in practice prepared for absolution.[420]

In addition, Victoria, who wrote before the year 1545, said:

But what is the confessor to do when both opinions are probable, and both have defenders? I respond that, whether one is talking about one's own parish priest or not, he is bound to give absolution in such a case…this is the view held by Paludanus.[421] It is clearly established; such a penitent is in grace, and the confessor has the probability that he is in grace, because he knows this is his own probable opinion. Thus, he should not deny him absolution.[422]

Adrianus writes in the same way:

If a contrary view is held by many, by serious writers, or even by the equal authority of doctors, the priest should not at that point presume he should hold to his own opinion and force it…given that his opinion could be erroneous.[423]

Navarrus says the same:

If there are contrasting opinions among the doctors...and the confessor thinks it is clear from the text that the mild opinion is correct but the penitent thinks it is a doubtful opinion, he ought not to absolve him....However, if the penitent is relying on an equal or nearly equal opinion and has some outstanding doctor on his side, he could absolve him.[424]

Then he adds: "If it is doubted whether the penitent ought to do or take this...the confessor ought to choose the more benign opinion."[425] In support of this view, he quotes Angelus and Silvestrus. The same view is confirmed by St. Antoninus in various places. In one of them he writes:

Goffredus de Fontibus seems to think in like manner, namely that in contrasting opinions that are allowed by the Church, as has been said, he ought to propose to the penitent that he should study the matter well, informing himself from prudent theologians and that some are studied who hold a different view, especially if the extraordinary confessor (thus, not the parish priest) be of the opposite opinion, and then he should absolve him. Bernard of Clairvaux thinks similarly but not distinguishing whether the confessor be the ordinary or extraordinary one.[426]

In another place the saintly archbishop, speaking of the contract (about which we spoke above) in a discussion in Florence, said that the person who wished to initiate the contract should be consulted, so that he might be dissuaded. He then adds: "What if the person refuses to take this advice?...It seems he should be left to his own judgment, nor should he be condemned on this account or denied absolution."[427] Elsewhere, however, he adds:

If truthfully the confessor cannot clearly see that it is a mortal sin...it would seem then that he should not come to a hasty judgment. This is what William the Speculator says on a similar matter, so that on this account he denies absolution, or makes the penitent conscious of the mortal sin....Afterward, acting against this, even if the matter in itself were not a mortal sin, for him it would be a mortal sin, because everything that is done against conscience leads to hell....Because it is easier to free from laws than to bind with them...it seems indeed that he should be absolved and sent on his way with a blessed judgment.[428]

As we noted above, John Gerson says the same: *doctors of theology ought not to be too quick in asserting that some sins are mortal when they are not most certain about the matter.* Note the words: *where they are not most certain.* In this way, authors of great note, whom no one would dare to accuse of being laxist, speak with one voice. Dominic Soto says: "The opinion of the penitent is probable and this excuses him from guilt; and thus he has the right of asking for absolution, which likewise, by asking, he is considered to have weighed up and pondered."[429] The same Soto says this in another place: "When there are probable opinions among serious doctors, you may follow any of them, and you will have a secure conscience."[430]

Finally, from everything that has been treated here, the principle handed on to us by St. Thomas has been confirmed: law, unless it is sufficiently and certainly promulgated, does not oblige. We conclude that we are not obliged to follow the law, unless the opinion that favors the law is certain or at least more probable. This is what we have been saying from the beginning.

PART TWO

Commentary on the *Treatise on Conscience*

INTRODUCTION TO COMMENTARY

Alphonsus wrote a moral theology for the students of his recently founded Redemptorist Congregation, with a first edition in 1748 and a ninth in 1785. Moral theology had developed after the Council of Trent (1545-1563) as a practical-oriented science to prepare ecclesiastical students for their future ministry as priests. Particular emphasis was given to the administration of the sacraments, principally confession. The theoretic framework of moral theology during this period was a legal one: divine law, natural law, human law, positive law, ecclesiastical law. Alphonsus wrote within that context of law, using an easy-to-follow exposition that would help students understand complex material. He starts with two observations.

The first one has pivotal importance. The starting point for their study is conscience. The exit point in pastoral ministry will also be through conscience. Alphonsus' moral theology had begun as a commentary on the work of another theologian, Hermann Busenbaum (1609-1668). The evolution of Alphonsus' thought over a thirty-year period is crystallized in this deliberate choice. The study of moral theology involves the various and distinctive levels of law, but it begins with an exploration of conscience. This is the characteristic feature of the Alphonsian organization of moral theology.

Some background, historical and ecclesiastical, helps one understand how Alphonsus analyzes conscience. There is no agreed-upon definition of the meaning of conscience. Besides, it is not a specifically Christian concept. Cicero, in *Pro Milo*, refers to conscience as the principal theater of virtue in life *(theatrum virtutis)*. One performs in that theater, for good or ill. Already recognized as a stimulus to action and an encouragement to change one's life, it was readily adaptable to Christian aspirations and needs. The Church embraced the drama of conscience enthusiastically in explaining what is involved in being a Christian. In the acceptance of conscience within Christian conversation, a comparatively small decision continues to be historically important. Jerome (347-420), in his translation of the New Testament, chose the Latin word *conscientia* for the Greek word *syneidesis*. The Greek word has connotations of looking inward, while the Latin word considers what is outside oneself. The self-awareness of *syneidesis* and the shared knowledge of *conscientia (cum scientia)* are different ways of looking at the reality we now refer to as conscience.

The significance of Jerome's translation does not seem to have created noteworthy ripples in the centuries immediately following him. Conscience was not a matter of much discussion in either philosophy or theology. This alters when feudal law was gradually replaced in Western Europe by Roman law. The effect of this on theology was to introduce an explanation of conscience as already having a content of its own validated by those with the authority to lay down and interpret the law. This gave rise to two claimants for the allegiance of a person: the inner voice of conscience, and the external word of those who commanded conscience. A series of problems developed, and not just for theology. Where conscience resides and has its home was the great dilemma for the poet William Langland in *Piers Plowman*, and the predicament throws a long shadow over the political and religious controversies of the Reformation period. Erasmus, Luther, Thomas More, and Henry VIII can all invoke conscience.

For the purpose of understanding our text, we need to appreciate why Alphonsus takes a particular direction from the options available to him. The choice was not conscience *or* law, but conscience *within* law. *Mea conscientia*, for Alphonsus, is not the lonely drama it was for Luther; it is played out within the community of the Church.

The second observation of the introductory memo is considerably more practical. Alphonsus quotes a lot of authors, and he outlines a procedure to distinguish their thinking from his own. Not all the references Alphonsus made are complete. His own thought evolved between different editions; printers were not always reliable. The text on which this translation is based (L. Gaudé, 1905) can, however, be taken as an accurate representation of Alphonsus' mature position on the question of conscience. The elimination of remaining errors can be left to future scholars prepared to dedicate themselves to a new critical edition. Meanwhile, the Gaudé edition is trustworthy for our purposes.

Commentary on Chapter One

ARTICLES 1-3
Conscience: definition and distinctions

AFFIRMING THAT THE STUDY OF MORAL THEOLOGY begins with the treatise on conscience is a comparatively straightforward claim. Understanding what Alphonsus recognizes as conscience will take us through the full journey of the treatise. He begins with three articles giving the basic terminology.

The moral life is a consideration of human actions. Moral theology is the professional science which trains us to do this. Human activity has many components, but Alphonsus' interest is in the moral decisions we take. There has to be a sure way of determining how these actions are to be considered good or evil. Of course, we have the eternal law of God. This could seem to be an adequate measure for deciding between good and evil actions. However, by placing conscience as the entry point for moral theology, Alphonsus insists on a second level for assessing the morality of human actions. They have to be looked at more closely, that is, from conscience. The two levels are connected in the sense that the divine law must be received by the individual conscience.

That is why the promulgation of the divine law in the individual conscience is a theological crux that will dominate the full treatise.

The *forma mentis* of Alphonsus was shaped by his training in jurisprudence. The law predates the case to be decided, and a final verdict of innocence or guilt is reached only after a consideration of all the circumstances. Here, of course, we are dealing with theology, not with jurisprudence, and the significance of the quotations from Thomas Aquinas should be noted. Conscience is not an alternative to divine law, but it is pivotal in deciding whether an action is to be considered good or bad. Alphonsus did not consider himself to be a commentator on Thomas Aquinas, like Cajetan or Suarez. The importance of Aquinas for him is to indicate the authority of his theological foundations. If there is support for the argument from Aquinas, Alphonsus is implying that his system can be trusted.

Alphonsus is considering one aspect of a complex question, the goodness or wrongness of a practical decision. This is decided on the basis of the good or bad will of the person acting. A moral judgment is based on the motivation within the particular action chosen. The acceptance of this point, in the first article of the treatise, is a noteworthy clarification of what Alphonsus means by taking conscience as the entry point for all moral theology. The citation from Aquinas indicates that Alphonsus considers his unfamiliar starting point to be coherent with the position of the most authoritative theologian in the Church.

The definition of conscience in Article 2 indicates where Alphonsus stands within the spectrum of other possible definitions. Conscience is a practical and reasonable judgment of what is to be done in the present moment. Calling it a practical judgment does not downgrade it, as if a conscience were merely practical and therefore not academically serious. The practical decision is, after all, something that is reached by reason, and Alphonsus is firmly within the theological tradition which respects human reason *(ratio)*. Where he differs from other theologians of his epoch is how he understands conscience as a different judgment to one reached through *synderesis*. This is a technical term from scholastic philosophy which refers to the inborn principle in the moral consciousness of every person. It directs the person toward good and restrains him from evil. Synderesis is a habit that shapes a person's general life. We can relate synderesis to the internal voice of conscience. The word is not much used now, and Joseph Cardinal Ratzinger suggested an interesting replacement in the idea of *anamnesis* (*On Conscience,* 1984) to indicate the memory of the voice of God in our heart. Alphonsus would have understood this. However, he chooses to define conscience as a separate act which is not to be confused with the habit-forming role of synderesis (or the memory-preserving role of anamnesis). The implication of the definition of conscience preferred by Alphonsus is that he neither considers the decision taken in conscience as a deduction from principles nor as an isolated inner light. Conscience occurs within the other aspects of life, but it is not to be confused with them. It is a separate act.

Generally speaking, a person must form the habit of thinking rightly. Synderesis is the technical term for doing this. Practically speaking, a person must take a decision in circumstances that are often far from ideal. Conscience is the guide for this. It is misleading to understand Alphonsus as saying that the theory learned by synderesis is then automatically applied to a particular situation. This impression has led some commentators to suggest that Alphonsus is proposing a double morality: one that is in accordance with theory, one that is tolerated in practice. Alphonsus knew very well that theory and practice rarely coincide. The difficulty is not with the truth of the morally right or wrong. The decisive question for Alphonsus is with the goodness or evil of the choice made by a particular person. When he insists that conscience is an act of practical judgment, as distinct from the speculative search for the truth of foundational principles, he is articulating a moral theology that can be serviceable in pastoral ministry. This is his purpose in writing his moral theology in the first place. He belongs to what we can generally call "the Thomistic tradition of theology." His questions, however, come from a pastoral context not normally considered by academic schools. This is very clear from his preface to *Theologia Moralis*. The freedom of the person faced with a decision is as important for Alphonsus as the truth implied in the decision eventually taken.

Alphonsus' personal approach becomes clearer in Article 3. Were he writing a moral theology for a specifically academic setting, this article would be about law and its many levels. Alphonsus, instead, outlines a sixfold division of conscience as he has defined it. His interest is in how the law is received and, pastorally speaking, this is determined in conscience.

Objectively, it is always a sin to act against a rightly formed conscience. Subjectively, it has to be established if the determination of sin applies in a particular instance. Analogous to the negative formulations in the Decalogue, it is easier to say what is forbidden ("do not kill") than to explain what is practically involved in a positive prescription ("keep holy the Sabbath day"). The conviction that it is objectively wrong, indeed a sin, to act against a properly formed conscience, and the complexity of knowing whether this is actually and subjectively wrong, is a recurrent issue of the treatise.

Alphonsus is not innovative in repeating what was standard teaching in the high Middle Ages: there is a distinction between an objective description and a subjective judgment in the moral life. His contribution is in the thoroughness with which he applies this traditional doctrine to circumstances not considered by the scholastics. He is concentrating on the subjective elements of morality within the ministry of the Church in the eighteenth century.

Though the language of Alphonsus about the types of conscience belongs to a different epoch, it is important to understand what the terminology would have meant for him. Only afterward can we assess whether the approach has relevance in a different era. Right conscience *(recta)* is based on the objectively proposed truth. The other five divisions proposed by Alphonsus are about the subjectively experienced states of the knowledge of the first truth. It is typical of Alphonsus to initially propose the ideal position and rather quickly move to the less-than-ideal situation. Law states the ideal to which one should conform. When this does not occur in practice, the solution is not to propose a new law but to seek a more precise understanding of why it was impossible in the first place for the person to have acted differently.

The truth that is given by the law is a truth that is clouded for a particular person. That is the logic of the presentation of the various states of conscience in Article 3. The Latin terms have a jurisprudential origin and are transposed here to a theological setting. Right *(recta)* gives the sense of being led along a correct path. That is the role of practical reason enabled by the law. Having stated that the ideal is that we would always lead an ordered life, Alphonsus turns his attention to a number of ways in which people may lose their footing on the preordained path. *Erronea* (translated as "erroneous") means "wandering around" in the sense of mistaking the right path. This is different from being *perplexa* (translated as "confused"). The person has not wandered from the right path, but is in a muddled or ambiguous state of mind. *Scrupulosa* (translated as "scrupulous") has its etymological origins in the idea of footwear being hampered by jagged stones. This will be treated at length in subsequent articles. Here the initial idea communicated is that the person wants to walk properly, but the scruples (the irritating stones) make this impossible. Different again is the conscience that is *dubia* (which I usually translate as "indecisive"). The person wavers and procrastinates, not knowing what to do. The final type of conscience is *probabile* (translated as "probable"). In Article 3 the term is used as an adjective. Later in the treatise Alphonsus will deal more extensively with the theory of probabilism.

The terminology is dated, legal in origin, and tied to casuistry. However, if we accept that conscience is an act of judgment that is distinct from the habit of forming a right-thinking mind, the approach of Alphonsus can continue to be functional. When we are taking a moral decision, we are deciding what is the proper thing to do in the present moment. With hindsight, we may realize that we have taken a wrong decision, but the rightness of the first decision stands. Though Alphonsus uses the standard division of objective and subjective morality, this distinction may not be as important as it seems. It is always the one human act that is considered by Alphonsus. We can look at this "remotely," as he suggests in the opening sentence of Article 1. We can also look at it "proximately," that is, through the lens of the decision of conscience. When Pope Francis asks, "Who am I to judge?" he is respecting the conscience of the person who will make the judgment. The presumption is that a judgment has to be made, and the only person who can make that judgment is the person involved. That is the significance of conscience considered as an act of practical judgment.

Besides quoting, in rather literalist ways, Scripture and Pope Innocent III, Alphonsus refers to fourteen theologians. This should be taken in the obvious sense of the serious study involved in reaching his conclusions. The key text is from the *De Veritate* of Thomas Aquinas. The other thirteen references are to theologians who wrote after Aquinas, many of them Jesuits. These statistical comments are indicative of the theological preferences of Alphonsus. He is more interested in recent theology because the problems he is dealing with are contemporary ones, and theologians of the Society of Jesus were among his favorites.

An erroneous conscience (that is, a conscience that is in error because it does not replicate in its decision the truth as given by the authoritative law) is a concept found in Thomas Aquinas. Alphonsus extends the understanding of Aquinas by giving lengthy attention to the reasons why one may act in error. The debate on the erroneous conscience in the last fifty years has not given much attention to this aspect of Alphonsus. The erroneous conscience is evidently connected with the truth of the matter. It is also related to the freedom of the person in making his or her choice, and it is the person's freedom that is of decisive import for Alphonsus. Some imply that the woes of the modern world are due to those who substitute the infallible (though erroneous) conscience for the clear objective teaching of authority. I have already given my view that Alphonsus' thinking is regulated by the framework of conscience-within-the-law. He pays proper attention to the erroneous conscience because it is simply a fact of life and has to be dealt with. In accepting the possibility of an erroneous conscience Alphonsus is also facing reality. He is not proposing an alternate and separate theory of morality outside the framework of law which dominates in his moral theology.

ARTICLES 4-5
Vincible and invincible ignorance

Two short articles elaborate on the importance of a crucial distinction made in the previous articles. No other author is referred to. These succinctly written articles represent Alphonsus' mature personal view on a substantial issue.

The starting point remains the fact that it is always a sin to act against a right conscience. The repetition of *peccat* (sins) three times in a few lines is indicative of the ministerial preoccupation of Alphonsus. Interpretations that he is sin-obsessed are, however, off the mark. In his logic, if a person wanders from the right path *(erronea)* in an unreasonable way, this is a sin. The use of the word *eligendo* (chooses) is significant because it underlines the need for interior consent of the will in judging what is a sin. Sin is not merely a material breaking of the law—one *chooses* to sin. It is not automatically to be equated with the material error *(erronea)*. Sin occurs when a reasonable effort to eliminate what one knows to be an error is not taken *(vincibilis)*.

Moral theology would be considerably easier if everything could be decided in terms of material knowledge. By choosing to start the study of moral theology with a treatise on conscience, Alphonsus is indicating that it is formal knowledge that is decisive in moral matters. If our ignorance can be overcome *(vincibilis)* we have a responsibility to act intelligently and correct the error. If, for whatever reason, we cannot overcome the error *(invincibilis)* then we cannot be held morally responsible in conscience. This is in line with the argument of Thomas Aquinas (*Summa Theologiae*, I II, q. 76). If ignorance is invincible, it means that it cannot be overcome even by reasonable effort; it is not a voluntary act because we have no power to overcome it within ourselves. I have translated the word *aliquando* as "at any given time" and "anytime." This has the sense of "always" *(semper)*. Alphonsus is aware that, judged by the remote rule of morality, an action may not be right. His preoccupation is with what is good as it appears to the proximate conscience of the acting person. *Aliquando* indicates the particular circumstances to be considered. A person is obliged to follow his conscience anytime he finds himself in these precise circumstances. In that sense, one is always obliged to follow the judgment of conscience.

These two articles are a keystone of the moral position of Alphonsus. They give the sense in which freedom and knowledge relate together in the carrying out of conscience. The tone of the articles is affirmative. The treatise will deal later with some of the complex arguments involved behind the assertions.

The debate about an erroneous conscience is a child of the adoption by theology of a system of Roman law over feudal and custom law. Conscience, considered as an inner voice, could come into conflict with conscience considered as what law demanded. Just as the notion of conscience itself did not have a univocal meaning in theology, it is understandable that the qualifying adjective "erroneous" depended on what one meant by the substance "conscience." Different explanations of an erroneous conscience have emerged and are still a matter of debate. Brian Johnstone (*Erroneous Conscience*, 114) has pointed out that there are distinctive emphases in the explanation of the erroneous conscience in *Gaudium et Spes* (1965), 16; *Veritatis Splendor* (1993), 63–64; and the *Catechism of the Catholic Church* (1994), 1786–1794. If there is no common definition of conscience, there will be different explanations of how it can be erroneous.

I am commenting on the text of Alphonsus and I do not propose to enter into debates that came after him. It is the debate which preceded him that is a better focus for understanding the text. Thomas Aquinas accepted two kinds of error in the consideration of conscience. One is an error about a circumstance; he considers this to be an involuntary error, and it is excusable. The second is an error about the law of God which one ought to know. Error is not an excuse about the law itself. However, is the person making a deliberate error (voluntary) or an unthinking error (involuntary)? A voluntary error cannot be excused; an involuntary one can. My understanding is that Alphonsus elaborates his system of moral theology within that schema, though he gives more attention to the practical circumstances of what is voluntary and involuntary than Aquinas does. Where Aquinas was considering the question of erroneous conscience in the context of the *aula*, Alphonsus was considering it in the *tribunale* of the confessional.

There is substantial consonance between the thinking of Thomas Aquinas and Alphonsus up to this point. However, a difference emerges between them in the consideration of the moral status of the action performed by the erroneous conscience. For Thomas, an involuntary erroneous conscience does not make such an act a good one, though it means the will is not evil (it is, after all, involuntary). For Alphonsus, not only does involuntary ignorance excuse from sin, but the will producing an act that is in conformity with an (invincibly) erroneous reason may in fact permit the act to be virtuous and meritorious.

ARTICLES 6-7
The question of merit

These two articles explain the position of Alphonsus and have, understandably, been the focus of much comment. Do they represent a coherently credible system of moral reasoning, or are they symptomatic of a confusion at the heart of the system?

Alphonsus is mindful of the implications of what he is saying. He calls it *probabilius* (more probable). For some of his opponents, what he says here is, quite simply, false because it forges an unacceptable partition between personal intention and the external action. There is no evidence in the text that Alphonsus tries to make artificial dissections of the one human act, though he certainly gives priority to intention in the assessment of the merit gained.

Article 6 is delicately phrased. Alphonsus repeats that, to act morally, a person should act prudently and reasonably. It is to be presumed that this type of person would not deliberately wish to lose his or her soul. Hence, a person can gain merit (grace) though the action chosen is wrong. Alphonsus quotes his contemporary Cuniliati. When he can, Alphonsus likes to quote favorably from a Dominican theologian of the period since, in general, the prominent theologians of the Order of Preachers were opposed to his system.

The argument does not initially focus on what is right or wrong but on whether a reasonable person can gain merit or, in a typical Alphonsian phrase, "wishes to be saved." Commentators who use these two articles to suggest that Alphonsus was incapable of understanding Aquinas miss the point. Alphonsus is dealing with a situation not immediately covered by texts from Aquinas. Article 6 is better understood as part of the theology of grace adopted by Alphonsus. God freely gives his grace to a person who desires to do good, just as he withholds grace from a person who acts with a wrong intention. The pastoral presumption is in favor of the goodwill of a person who wishes to be saved. Bad choices may be made, but these will not necessarily destroy the good intention. Equally, and tellingly, a good action cannot supplant a deliberately wrong intention.

If Article 6 is best interpreted within the theology of grace, Article 7 revolves around a more characteristic moral axis—the relationship between the object and the subject in a moral decision. The text, as we now have it, dates from the sixth edition (1767) and reflects the decades-long toil of Alphonsus for clarity in his moral system. It is noticeable that, when he regards an opinion as more probable, he often follows by quoting authors who would not normally agree with him, as is the case here with Franzoja and Concina. They were contemporaries of Alphonsus, but did not share his views on the use of the probable opinion. The dry comment that even the Dominican Concina "is now close to our view" would not have been lost on contemporary readers who were interested in the debate.

The answers to the objections center on Alphonsus' understanding that the truth of the judgment of conscience is based on a circumstance-related discernment. Alphonsus implies that the first citation from Aquinas is not applicable to the type of moral dilemma he is dealing with. The practical judgment of conscience is guided by the good perceived in reality; it is not a judgment that can be automatically deduced from speculative theory. It is a separate act of judgment, different from the conclusions that might be deduced from a more conceptual argument.

The quotation from St. Bernard should be understood as a typical device of Alphonsus, used in other genres of his writings. It is an example (exemplum) which makes an argument more concrete through a story or incident.

Debates about the interpretation of the texts from Aquinas cited in Article 7 will continue. The bigger issue involves more than this textual question. It is related to an understanding of grace or merit, introduced in Article 6. We cannot merit salvation by good works, nor can we be deprived of salvation if our will (voluntarium) is seeking conformity to what God wills for us. This judgment, made in conscience, is best left to the God in whose presence the decision is finally made.

The Second Vatican Council's Dogmatic Constitution on the Church (Lumen Gentium), 16, is interesting in the way it broadens the question that Alphonsus faces here:

COMMENTARY ON CHAPTER ONE

There are those who without any fault do not know anything about Christ or his Church, yet who search for God with a sincere heart and under the influence of grace, and try to put into effect the will of God known to them in the dictate of conscience: these too can obtain eternal salvation.

I mention this to indicate that the focus on a technical text from Aquinas, which has been at the center of much controversy about Alphonsus, could be expanded. Nonculpable ignorance is not only a moral statement, as *Lumen Gentium* 16 allows. Salvation is the deeper question which needs consideration. The technical relationship between "object" and "subject" in moral discourse is important, but in a relative sense. How we can be saved at all is the weightier question that preoccupies Alphonsus.

ARTICLES 8-9
Clarifications on invincible ignorance

Article 8 is concise. This treatise is about conscience, but there is a larger topic for the student to master: moral theology. The treatise on laws will take the student into that. Pedagogically, this article alerts the student to the fact that conscience, for all its importance as the decisive entry point, is not the same as the mastery of the full science of moral theology.

Moral theology, as understood in the time of Alphonsus, involved a study of principles: first principles, secondary principles, reflex principles. These terms will be explained more fully later. At this stage, it is sufficient to appreciate the centrality of law in Alphonsus' moral theology. This is not exclusively a result of his legal training, though it surely includes this. As a seminarian,

Alphonsus had been trained during the period of second scho-
lasticism, which gave prominent attention to law. In his moral
writing, Alphonsus implicitly follows an Aristotelian rather than
a Platonic construct of law. Law is a rational basis for behavior
in particular circumstances rather than an ideal that is proposed
and which can be interpreted only by the authority prescribing
the law. Too much can be made out of an unsophisticated juxtaposition between Aristotelian and Platonic traditions. There is
no doubt, however, that the overall Aristotelian position which
leaves room for a consideration of circumstances in the interpretation of law appealed to the pastorally concerned Alphonsus.
The reference to Thomas Aquinas is from the *Summa Theologiae*
Ia IIae, q. 76. This would be a central text for his students later in
their studies, as Alphonsus states that what he is saying here is
"proved" by Aquinas *(probabimus)*. The headings of the inquiry
in Aquinas' text are: (a) does ignorance cause sin (b) is ignorance
sinful (c) does ignorance excuse us completely from sin and (d)
does ignorance lessen sin. The students would be expected to
study this text when they come to the tract on laws. Alphonsus
hints at this, but at this point does not wish to lose his focus on
the issue of conscience.

This becomes clearer with the changed tone of the writing in
Article 9. It might well reflect a discussion with Alphonsus during
the "moral cases" which were an obligatory part of community
life among the early Redemptorists. Though the tone is colloquial
("you may say," "you might continue") and the main example was
likely to attract interest (fornication), the argument on the difference between internal and external sin is specialized. The article
is a striking example of how moral theology deals with very practical matters of conscience but, in the absence of serious study on
the underlying concerns, one could come to defective solutions.

The distinction between internal and external sin brings

Alphonsus back to an insistence on *lumen* (light, as in divine enlightenment) with respect to *ratio* (reason) and *ius naturalis* (the law we have by nature). While the focus of this article continues to be the distinction between vincible and invincible ignorance, at the level of law, Alphonsus raises another question that should be considered. His technical comments on the relationship between light and reason are basic to explaining that desire *(desiderium)* is more properly located in the will *(voluntas)* where the question of ignorance of law is not the central focus. The freedom of the will is fundamental to the exposition of Thomas Aquinas on the question; the freedom of the decision taken in practice is fundamental to the exposition of Alphonsus.

If Article 9 was written in the light of community discussions on moral cases, as I consider possible, the above comments would very likely not have been received enthusiastically by confreres who wanted to get straight to the question—fornication. The point of discussing cases, for Alphonsus, is not necessarily to provide answers (he gives remarkably few, actually) but to clarify how one thinks through an issue in order to come to secure solutions in practical moral cases.

The relationship between the will and intellect (*voluntas, ratio*) in making moral judgments remains a most difficult issue to explain. Learned theses are still being written on the topic (Hugh Clifford: *The Relationship between the Intellect and the Will in the Moral Theology of St. Thomas*, Alphonsian Academy, 2018). Alphonsus gives considerable weight to the role of reason in moral judgment, without allowing himself to be trapped in a rationalist cul-de-sac. He accepts the place of the will as fundamental, without being hemmed into a nominalist cage. In terms of the argument as presented in this article, it is noteworthy how Alphonsus wishes to demonstrate that the *object* of the will is more properly defined in terms of the *internal* act of the will. It is the light of reason, communicated to the will, which defines what is a properly human act.

Alphonsus is clear that sin, formally so called, cannot be identified with a material act. He takes care to show that, while this is true, human desire has to be judged in a different light, literally. When he is commenting on a difficult and delicate issue, as the relationship between reason and will surely is, it is interesting to observe how the solution that emerges for him is from pastoral experience, as is the case in Article 9.

Alphonsus had significant interest in technical issues raised by scholastic theology, such as the question of *voluntas* and *ratio*. His exchanges with Dominican theologians are a testimony. His deeper passion, however, is how these questions affect pastoral practice. It is to be recalled, again, that Alphonsus is writing for beginners in the science of moral theology. The entry point is conscience, because the exit point for the students will also be conscience when they are engaged in apostolic work. Serious study of moral theology is required if one is to progress from conscience to conscience.

Article 9 reflects the state of a question in the time of Alphonsus, though it retains interest for some modern and unresolved issues about human will, action, and desire. This could be especially true in the psychosexual area. The example for Alphonsus is fornication. The arrival of cybersex and sexual addictions involves analogous issues of intention, action, and desire.

The approach indicated in Articles 8 and 9 resonates with what Pope Francis says:

> Doing what is right means more than "judging what seems best" or knowing clearly what needs to be done, important as this is. Often we prove inconsistent in our

own convictions, however firm they may be. Even when our conscience dictates a clear moral decision, other factors sometimes prove more attractive and powerful. We have to arrive at a point where the good that the intellect grasps can take root in us in a profound affective inclination (On Love in the Family [Amoris Laetitia], 265).

Good moral decisions are based on proper reasoning, and positive education helps us appreciate that the practical decisions we take need to be good, not just in theory, but for ourselves personally. Pope Francis does not quote Alphonsus in Amoris Laetitia, but I notice a shared thread in their understanding of some texts of Aquinas. There is also a link between the two in their appreciation that reality is more important than ideas.

ARTICLE 10
The perplexed conscience

Alphonsus is a casuist within the tradition of jurisprudence that he studied at the University of Naples. Article 10 is a thought-provoking example of the training of Alphonsus in jurisprudence and how he transfers this to a theological context. In a legal case there is, by its nature, perplexity. Two or more opinions can be offered in a court case. The judgment has to demonstrate why one opinion is preferred over another. To avoid an arbitrary approach to law, the only way to justify a preference is by an appeal to principles, gradating them according to their importance in a particular case. Alphonsus does precisely this in explaining the different weight to be given to natural, human, and positive divine law.

The article uses a principled casuistry for the solution of a moral case. I would underline, however, how Alphonsus closes the discussion with a reference to the necessity of freedom in the consideration of formal sin. Trained in jurisprudence, comfortable in the resolution of cases, Alphonsus also articulates a theological argument. Freedom is always pivotal to the conscience-oriented moral theology of Alphonsus.

I do not believe that using the argumentation implied in Article 10 necessarily makes one a casuist, in the uncomplimentary sense. Such casuistry should have no place in moral theology. That acknowledged, I draw attention to the fact that Alphonsus is careful to be specific about the issue at stake (in this article, the person is perplexed, which is different from being ignorant or having an erroneous conscience). The details enable him to choose which principles to apply in a particular situation. I can think of analogies today where people are more perplexed about what to do than in outright bad faith about morality.

ARTICLES 11-18
Scruples

Nine articles, almost half the entire chapter, deal with scruples. This could strike a contemporary reader as surprising and unbalanced. Why the need for such an extensive treatment? At the level of pastoral ministry, the effects of Jansenism in theology and rigorous morality in preaching and sacramental practice left a substantial legacy of guilt-induced scrupulosity. The missionary Alphonsus considered its eradication to be an apostolic priority. At the level of personal character, there is evidence that Alphonsus was bothered by repeated bouts of scrupulosity.

Accepting these general motivations, and without analyzing them further at this point, I would prefer to highlight how the moral logic of these articles is consistent with the previous ones.

By presenting conscience as the entry point for all of moral theology, Alphonsus chooses to focus on the immediate and practical judgment of the act of conscience. Reason (*ratio*) is the consistent characteristic of such judgments. The four signs of scrupulosity (Article 11) relate to the lack of reasonable judgment in practice. Scrupulosity is an illness. Alphonsus focuses on how this illness affects one's judgment in moral and spiritual matters. However, the text allows us to understand this illness in a broad sense. Scrupulosity is not the preserve of religious people. The sickness of scruples, in whatever facet of life, is an inability to act freely and prudently. Psychological and psychiatric studies on scruples will use terminology consistent with their disciplines. If the illness is considered from a moral and religious aspect, the signs of scrupulosity given by Alphonsus can still be recognized.

The ministerial and personal motivations for dealing at such length with scruples becomes clearer with Article 12. The writing style is expository. In the early part of the article, there are five rules of thumb to recall in practice. In the latter part, there are ten quotations from other authors. A response could be that this hardly merits being called an argument; it is a list of practical points boosted by a string of quotations loosely threaded together. Given what Alphonsus says about scruples as an illness, a different assessment is possible.

Alphonsus, considering scruples as the incapacity to reason sensibly, emphasizes authorities who can be trusted. Did Alphonsus keep a list of the quotations and the practical advice near at hand, for his own use? Quite likely. The quotations are from spiritual masters and experienced pastors, unlike the more speculative theologians cited in other articles. The sense of Article 11, in terms of the overall treatise, displays the practicality of the understanding of conscience in Alphonsus. The emphasis on obedience to a director/confessor, and distinctions between higher and lower parts of the soul, are from a different theological age. It would not be a contemporary method of clarification. In the case of Alphonsus, the phrasing underlines the necessity of reasonably accepted authority. In moral decisions, one needs a level of certainty. The scrupulous person, by himself, cannot reach that certainty. Relying on the authority of a confessor/director can be, within the logic of Alphonsus, a reasonable choice to make.

It is not surprising that Alphonsus gives priority to the loss of eternal salvation as the greatest predicament for scrupulous people (Article 13). We should note, however, his insistence that scruples can lead to mental imbalance, physical illness, depression, and suicide. The fact that these are not put at the same level as loss of salvation hardly lessens their importance in the practical support of a scrupulous person.

Recalling that these articles deal with the practical understanding of the judgment of conscience, the reference to prudence in Article 14 is significant. Alphonsus frequently refers to the first of the cardinal virtues in a specific way. The confessor is prudent by observing his different roles in their correct order. These roles are best explained in Alphonsus' *Praxis Confessarii*, a work incorporated into the later editions of the moral theology. Common sense in sacramental practice is never to be underestimated. Alphonsus mentions how even the most polite confessor can be worn out by scrupulous people badgering and exasperating them. Even the rigidly inclined Dominican Concina knows this.

Articles 15 and 16 reflect the experience of Alphonsus as a confessor. Jansenism and rigorous moralism were prevalent. Their effect on sensitive people contributed to an increase in the illness of scrupulosity. The fundamental appeal of Alphonsus is to the authority of the confessor (that is, for him, of God). How applicable this might be in a different world of differing cultural experiences is not immediately obvious. It remains useful to be reminded that "bad thoughts" are not the problem, but the consent given to them. This brings us back to the necessity of freedom for formal sin. This emphasis retains its importance. The terror-inducing tactics of former times may have disappeared. The dominance of sexualized imagery in contemporary life can cause another sort of scruple-related anxiety for sensitive people. The Alphonsian acknowledgment of freedom as necessary for sin remains valid in this context.

Of the six authors referred to in Article 16, only one (Wigandt) is given a precise reference by Alphonsus. The views of the others were so embedded in his thought processes that he may well have memorized them. The outstandingly diligent Gaudé traces them in his 1905 edition. The pastoral necessity to carefully distinguish differing circumstances in divergent cases comes through in this article. It is also a noteworthy example of how Alphonsus, benign in his general moral disposition, can be quite strict when circumstances require. Scrupulosity is an illness; the confessor, as a healer, should take a stern line with those who do not take their prescribed medicine. Integrity of confession refers to the canonical requirement to confess sins according to their number, kind, and species. Formal integrity is more important than material integrity. Scrupulosity is such a debilitating illness that the need for integrity in any sense can be eliminated. The scrupulous person would not be able to recognize the difference between material and formal integrity.

Two Articles, 17 and 18, put the preceding experience-based comments in a more structured way. The significant line of reasoning in Article 17 is how Alphonsus relates the problem of scruples to a disturbed power of reasoning *(ob rationem pertur-batam)*. The emphasis on obedience is to be understood against this background; it is the only way a scrupulous person can retain sanity. The illness of scrupulosity affects all of a person's life. Spiritual progress is affected, also physical and mental health. It is not necessary to conclude that Alphonsus advocates blind obedience as a general norm; he is encouraging a purposeful obedience in a particular context. Only when a person can think rationally can they act freely *(libere)* on the basis of what is apparent *(evidens)*. Modern psychological theories can surely add to our expertise on these matters. Alphonsus is concentrating on the moral problem of religious scruples at a particular period. Deprived of the capacity for rational argument and judgment, scrupulous people lack the freedom necessary for sin.

It is this freedom that is the thread of the argument in Article 18. If a person is in error, or doubtful about the goodness of an action, no judgment can be made until the error or doubt is cleared up. I noted in my comments on the opening articles that Alphonsus wrote the treatise on conscience to explain the practical rather than the theoretical character of moral action. This is the background to the emphasis on *honestas* rather than *bonum* in deciding the goodness of an action. The correct understanding of doubt *(dubium)* is critical. A doubt is legitimate when the precept to be applied is derived from an imperfect norm—for instance, a norm that has not been properly promulgated or has been abrogated. A legitimate doubt, consequently, justifies not applying a norm. The question then becomes: Can a legitimate doubt be caused by scruples? Alphonsus answers in the affirmative, offering the significant observation that the mind, being clouded by scruples, cannot think properly. A doubt can have its origin in the illness of scruples.

The quotations from Concina and Pope Benedict XIV are quite deliberate. Theologians looking for shoddy or lax views in Alphonsus during his life, and there were a lot of them, would have had access to the writings of Concina and the Pope. Both of these would have been considered "safe" by Alphonsus' opponents. To be able to quote from such authors gave greater plausibility to his argument. Alphonsus became increasingly sensitive about his moral views as he grew older. The crisis around the suppression of the Society of Jesus, which was in place in Portugal by 1759, was a worrying sign that proponents of the probable view in moral theology were losing the battle. Some of Alphonsus' own confreres, particularly those in Sicily, were putting pressure on him to tone down his own probable views. He resisted this, and being able to quote from Concina and the Pope was shrewd.

It is ironic how Alphonsus is sometimes quoted to propose a rigorous morality of the type he strove to eradicate. The text of these articles is obviously time-bound, and I would not be confident in proposing them literally in our time. That said, the pastoral spirit of Alphonsus in dealing with the complexity of scruples could be recovered, with benefit, by pastoral ministers.

ARTICLE 19
The foundation of a judgment of conscience

The structure of Article 19 is characteristically Alphonsian. He begins by insisting that his interest is in practice *(pro praxi)* and he finishes by asserting that, other things being equal, the benign opinion is to be preferred over a rigid one. These are the bookends within which a distinctive line of argument is advanced.

It is important to emphasize that it is an argument. Affirming that Alphonsus is "practical" or "benign" is of little use, unless we understand the how and why of the claim that is being made. This article argues that the critical element in the formation of conscience is the judgment of reason *(sentenia rationis)* and the process of this formation involves discernment *(deliberatio)*. The problems studied in this part of the treatise are particular (scrupulosity) but the argument has a wider range (a formed conscience). When a conscience is unstable *(inter dubia vacillat)*, there is no hope of reaching a reasonable judgment. Without a reasonable judgment, there is no proper basis for freedom in a moral action. Without freedom, there is no morality.

Alphonsus offers no easy or automatic technique for the formation of conscience. The process of reasonable discernment indicated presumes an internal consistency that can be obscured by making a forced distinction between a formed and an informed conscience. The anthropological basis of the theology of Alphonsus is a biblical consideration of the person made in the image of God. A formed conscience is a human activity that implicitly includes a spiritual dimension. The distinction between a formed conscience and an informed conscience which has been made in theological literature in recent decades is not one that I can find in the Alphonsian text. A conscience is formed by a process that presumes an integral consideration of the person. Clearly, we live in a different age and Church to that of Alphonsus. The ease with which Alphonsus speaks of the spiritual dimension of the human person is more difficult to express now. In one aspect, however, there is a commonality between the epoch of Alphonsus and ours. In both, the core of a formed conscience is an interior journey. False distinctions about the formation of conscience, observed exteriorly, are to be avoided.

The choice of the main author quoted (Jean Gerson, 1363-1429) is significant. He had some views that Alphonsus would not have shared. Gerson, for instance, accepted the superiority of a general council over a pope; Alphonsus was a staunch defender of papal power and infallibility. What appealed to Alphonsus was Gerson's general insistence on the practicality of theological discourse, the inner link between spiritual and moral progress, and the need to keep theological language as accessible as possible. Gerson was much bothered by the meaning of moral certainty. This was a dramatic question during the period of the Great Schism. Gerson could not appeal to the authority of an infallible pope to settle a dispute, because he could not be sure who was pope. Life had to go on, concrete decisions had to be made, and the proposal of moral certainty as a basis for practical decisions in conscience is a historically important legacy from Gerson. Moral certainty developed a different timbre by the time of Alphonsus. What he incorporates from Gerson is most applicable to solve the typical moral uncertainties of Southern Italy in the eighteenth century. It could still be useful as the debate about moral certainty takes a new twist in an age of fake news and alternative facts.

This chapter began with a definition of conscience in Article 2. It is interesting to return to this definition after Article 19 and note how pastoral experience gives a more precise expression to the essential Alphonsian approach to the practical judgment of conscience.

Commentary on Chapter Two

ARTICLES 20-21
Conscience and doubts

CHAPTER ONE OPENED WITH A PEDAGOGICAL EX-POSITION of terminology to explain conscience and concluded with a vindication of how the practical judgment of conscience is always binding. Chapter Two also opens with a presentation of key terms, this time from moral theology. After the Council of Trent (1545-1563), this science developed as a seminary-based ecclesiastical course in training candidates for priesthood. Law was the accepted anchor of this recent science. For Alphonsus, conscience opens the door into understanding how it functions in practice.

The doubts presented in these opening articles are related, in one way or another, to moral theology as an organized discipline of study. Conscience, by itself and according to its own character, is infallible. Doubts and hesitations can be imposed on conscience from the construct of law within which moral theology functioned. These doubts of law are complicated by doubts of fact in making a judgment in a particular situation. Writing, as he was, for students, Alphonsus avoids overly technical discussions at this stage. However, some knowledge of these debates was necessary for the student of the eighteenth century. We, too, need to become familiar with the terminology.

Though all moral theologians in Alphonsus' time accepted a legal paradigm for the science, there were differing systems explaining how this operated in the reality of Christian life. The extremes are easily identified: rigoristic imposition of the law that in effect allowed no room for discernment, permissive acceptance of any view that in effect excluded consideration of binding norms. Characteristically, Alphonsus avoids both extremes. He developed a system of the probable opinion to provide the adequate certainty which conscience needs in coming to a necessary decision. The probable opinion will be discussed more fully in Chapter Three. This chapter deals with preliminary, though important, questions. Doubts must be eliminated before one comes to a probable level of moral certainty. The distinction between negative and positive doubts lays out the boundaries to achieve this.

The distinction between negative and positive doubts, important in jurisprudence is of lesser significance in moral theology. The distinction between speculative and practical doubt (Article 3) is of greater consequence. Speculative doubt *(dubium speculativum)* refers to theoretical uncertainty; intellectually one does not know the truth of the matter. Alphonsus is concerned with practical doubt *(dubium practicum)*. This reinforces the position, clear from Chapter One, that conscience is a practical judgment, different from a speculative judgment. Doubts of a speculative nature can affect the practical judgment, but only indirectly *(licet in obliquo)*.

The examples in Article 21 make this more concrete, though the structure of the implicit argument is intricate. It hinges on the relationship between *veritas, honestas,* and *licitus.* I translate *veritas* as truth and *licitus* as lawful (or, occasionally, licit). The most difficult of the words to translate into English is *honestas.* Moral probity is central to the concept, and it also implies goodness of character and rightness in action (a person can be called "honest" in both senses). The view of *honestas* in St. Ambrose has influenced my effort to convey the sense of *honestas* in the text of Alphonsus. Ambrose contrasts *honestas* with *utile.* Nothing is really "useful" unless it is first "honest"; nothing is "honest" unless it corresponds to the "truth" that is at stake.

How to arrive intelligently at what is lawful *(licitum)* is the issue for Alphonsus. It is a miscalculation to see him coming to a judgment about what is licit in the trimmed-down terms of accepting something solely because it is legally allowable. Alphonsus does not belong to the voluntarist school associated with Occam (circa 1287-1347) which justifies what is permissible *(licit)* by reference to the authority allowing it. Alphonsus is unquestionably within the casuist tradition, but his argument is more often than not based on intrinsic calculation (from *veritas* through *honestas* to *licitum*). Obligation is innate to the person, and the imposition of an external obligation on an apparently indeterminate person is not his approach. While it is the *licitum* that is the point of arrival for him, the prior stages of *veritas* and *honestas* are given appropriate importance.

Alphonsus is not offering a speculative account of truth as Thomas Aquinas does in *De Veritate.* He is considering a different question about truth in practice. However, Alphonsus stays within the practical reasoning of the tradition of Aquinas rather than the voluntarist framework favored by followers of Occam.

ARTICLES 22-24
Practical doubts

The language of these articles is that of eighteenth-century moral theology. The doubts which arise for conscience were largely created by a particular theory (moral theology) rather than by conscience itself. The specter of scruples is never far away, as is nearly always the case when Alphonsus writes about doubts.

Article 22 is peremptory. Modern exegetes would question the use of the citation from the Book of Ecclesiasticus. This is now generally taken as a comment on wisdom versus foolishness and not sin, as Alphonsus would have understood that term.

A central issue in establishing the sense of Article 23 is the understanding of *objectum* in the determination of sin. Does the object of a moral act reside in the species alone, or can it include a consideration of the person performing the action? Indications in the last part of this article are persuasive about giving attention to the situation of the person in doubt. The contemporary debate about objective morality versus subjective morality is foreign to the mindset of Alphonsus. However, the way in which *objectum* is used in the second last sentence is an indication that Alphonsus considers the object of a moral decision to be within the state of mind of a person. The sinfulness of what the person chooses is not predetermined by the external (objective) species. The last sentence of Article 23 has a personal tone, as if Alphonsus were considering his own position.

The line of argument is presented in Articles 22-23 and rounded off in Article 24. A person cannot act in conscience if there is practical doubt, and when there is such a doubt it must be resolved. An effort should be made by the person using their intelligence to work their way out of the indecisiveness. If this is not possible, extrinsic authority can be appealed to. Even if the possibilities of an intrinsic or extrinsic resolution of the practical doubt have been exhausted, there could be one further consideration. We may be in the domain of involuntary ignorance. At this point, there can be no question of sin for the reason that sin always implies a voluntary act.

The technical language of Article 24 is from the epoch's conception of moral theology. However, the underlying issue of moral certainty remains a concern for our time, even if we operate with another interpretation of moral theology.

How does a person resolve uncertainty in practice? This is the substantial issue and will be with us for the rest of the chapter. Using principles that are certain is the first way indicated. However, such principles are few (*do good and avoid evil,* and the like). They will be of little use in the complexities of a knotty situation, especially for a person who is immature or poorly educated. This is the background to the use of reflex principles in the resolution of practical doubts. Article 26 will deal with this more thoroughly. Here I offer an initial comment:

If a doubt cannot be eliminated by direct certain principles or through intrinsic practical reasoning, then one can have recourse to indirect principles. These are properly called reflex principles because they reflect (as in a mirror) what can be known from direct principles. It should be obvious that solutions reached through reflex principles are not precise mathematical solutions to a query. Moral decisions are more complex than deductions from a syllogism.

Once again, the text reflects the legal training of Alphonsus. In law, not everything is certain and there must be supplementary processes to resolve doubts that may arise. The difference between legal certainty and moral certainty is, however, important to highlight. The external forum of the law can extend the legal procedures if all doubts are not resolved in the first instance. The doubt is referred to a higher court for a legal interpretation. In moral theology, if doubts are not resolved in the first instance, the appeal is not to reinvoke the law, but to resolve the issue where the doubt now resides—the conscience of a person. Against this decision of conscience, there is no appeal. That is why we need the optimum principles (reflex principles) to resolve doubts of conscience. The law deals with what is right or wrong in the public forum; morality is about the goodness of a decision *(honestas)* in the internal forum. The maxim *philosophia ancilla theologiae* (philosophy is the servant of theology) is less true of Alphonsus than *jurisprudentia ancilla theologiae moralis* (jurisprudence is the servant of moral theology).

ARTICLE 25
Speculative doubts

Three articles on practical doubts are followed by a single one on speculative doubts. The order and length of treatment reveal the priorities of Alphonsus. Article 25 is an expansion of what has been already said in Article 21. Though brief, the distinctions made are significant for understanding the whole treatise. The argument hinges on how Alphonsus understands the relationship with and the distinction between truth considered in itself, goodness in action, and liceity *(de rei veritate, de honestate actionis, licitum)*. Veracity *(de rei veritate)* is the starting point; this is largely speculative as one seeks to establish the truth of something. Having determined this, as far as humanly possible, a person moves on to reasoning about the goodness of the action chosen *(de honestate actionis)* on the basis of whether it is lawful or not *(licitum)*. A hierarchy of importance is established in understanding how conscience functions. The relationship between the levels of speculative truth, moral goodness, and lawfulness has notable consequences. Of equivalent significance is the distinction between them. Abstract truth has a priority at the level of speculation; goodness and liceity have a priority in action. The judgment taken in conscience is a separate act, different to that of theory. Thus, for Alphonsus, the judgment of conscience is not the plain application of a theory to practice. It is a distinct act of judgment considered in itself.

ARTICLE 26-27
Reflex principles

Having outlined his understanding of practical and speculative doubt, Alphonsus explains in more detail what is meant by reflex principles. These help to solve the practical problems of what is certain in conscience. Alphonsus is not introducing new moral "truths"; he is explaining a principled procedure to solve dilemmas of a practical nature in making a judgment of conscience.

The legal training of Alphonsus is very noticeable in these articles. I offer my understanding of the legal terms, followed by how they are transferred to moral theology.

Possession is the central legal term that recurs throughout the articles (*conditio possidentis, possessio, possidet, possessor*). Whoever owns something has the trump card in legal disputes. Possession is not only nine-tenths of the law; it becomes everything, from the point of view of justice and morality. When a person is born, his first possession is literally freedom. Morality cannot bind a person while the condition of original freedom continues. We are bound by the freedom in which we are born. This cannot be taken away from us except by a certain and promulgated law which then takes "possession" of the place previously held by freedom.

Doubts *(dubia)* arise when it may not be clear whether the law has been sufficiently promulgated or perhaps even abrogated. These doubts are of key importance, since they concern the fundamental idea of freedom. Reflex principles are borrowed from jurisprudence to reach moral certainty in such dilemmas.

Presumption *(praesumptio)* is a further step in the legal-to-moral exposition of Alphonsus. In jurisprudence, presumption comes into play when the law determines an unproven fact from another one that is certain and known. If the presumption is correctly demonstrated, then a person becomes the bona fide possessor or owner of whatever is at stake (property in civil law, liceity in church law).

A contemporary reader may be initially unconvinced by this type of argument for the range of moral dilemma our post-truth world presents. We will come to that challenge later. My intention here is to explain how the legal *forma mentis* of Alphonsus was transposed to moral theology as he understood that science. During his training in jurisprudence, Alphonsus learned how to bring legal finality to an argument. Turning to moral theology, Alphonsus is concerned about how to reach moral finality in a judgment. There is a continuing respect for law in the two vocations of Alphonsus. Besides, in view of his missionary purpose in founding the Redemptorists, he develops an increasing commitment to explaining how law functions as a defense advocate for the accused. There is a tribunal dimension to the conscience-law tension in the writings of Alphonsus. We need to accept this, though it is not the only dimension as we appreciate from his other works, like the *Praxis Confessarii*.

The reflex principles are not to be understood as crafty ways of circumventing the law. They are a procedural means by which the rights of the defendant are respected. When Alphonsus is advocating for the position that conscience is the entry point for moral theology (the substance of the whole treatise) he is taking a rhetorical as much as a logical stance. This perspective colors my assessment of the legal terminology of these articles.

> Now the object of rhetoric, says Aristotle, is judgment. Rhetoric differs from logic which can appeal to the rules of logical inference as the ultimate arbiter of truth. Rhetorical arguments must have access to a much wider range of appeals because of the variations among those who will sit in judgment. If the audience to which an argument is directed judges it to be a failure, it fails—however logically coherent it may be. By rhetorical standards, an argument succeeds only when the audience is persuaded (D. Cunningham, *Faithful Persuasion*, 44).

Article 27 could have appeared, almost word by word, in a legal textbook of the eighteenth century. *Condita* refers to the formulation of a law (technically, by the *conditores*, those who frame the law). A doubt can arise at this level, for instance: Can one be sure whether those who formulated the law had, in fact, the authority to do so? Presumption comes into the equation when one moves from a known law or fact to an unknown one. The legal maxim *praesumptio cedit veritate* (presumption defers to truth) is not used in the text, but it is taken for granted. In contemporary usage, "presumption" has a weak meaning ("that's only a presumption"). For Alphonsus it has a stronger connotation because of its specific legal sense.

Articles 26-27 imply a legal-to-moral explanation of reflex principles. For Alphonsus, they are principles to resolve doubts in practice. They should never be invoked as truth-generating principles themselves. They are a means to the end of reaching the practical certainty which is necessary for a decision in conscience.

There are other concerns to be taken into account when assessing the comprehensive moral argument of the overall treatise. For now, it is enough to appreciate why Alphonsus uses reflex principles as part of his system.

ARTICLES 28-30
Private vows

These articles reflect the social mores of eighteenth-century Italy. Personal vows were common and taken with great seriousness, often invoking the help of God, our Lady, or some favored saint to guarantee the fulfillment of a vow. Alessandro Manzoni's *The Betrothed* (1825-27) is an attractive literary account of this type of world. A vow was understood as analogous to a law imposed on oneself. It is interesting to note in Article 29 how Alphonsus changed his view when intrinsic reasoning becomes stronger than extrinsic authority. The treatise, with its many references, can give an impression of extrinsic reasoning. Many authors are indeed quoted, though the position of Alphonsus on a particular question is never decided by numbers. This article is an example of how he read widely but with an eye to clarifying the underlying line of reasoning in a question. It is ironic how Alphonsus himself came to be used as an external arbiter in moral arguments, particularly in the period between his proclamation as doctor of the Church (1871) and being conferred with the title Patron of Confessors in 1950. Advice he gave to early confreres was not always followed by later ones: "I do not mean that my opinions must necessarily be followed but I implore you, before you reject them, to read my book and ponder carefully what I have written with so much effort, thought, and study" (Letters, Vol. 3, 260).

These articles have a contemporary interest insofar as they

confirm, by analogy with law, how moral certainty is to be reached when a person has a doubt. The last section of Article 30 shows how certainty is located within the will of a person. If conscience is an infallible judgment, doubts about its obligatory force have to be resolved where those doubts appear, that is, within the conscience of the person. Moral certainty is neither a mathematical process for an individual nor can it be outsourced to authorities extrinsic to the person.

ARTICLES 31-34
The resolution of various cases

These articles are of restricted importance for understanding the general argument of the treatise (conscience) or the specific matter of this chapter (conscience and doubt). The cases dealt with (obedience in Article 31, fasting in Article 32, marriage in Article 33, paying a debt in Article 34) are so conditioned by canonical legislation of the period that entering into them in detail would be a distraction from my purpose in this commentary. A general comment will suffice.

Casuistry is never a substitute for proper moral reasoning. How the art of casuistry developed needs, however, to be placed in its historical context. In its classic form it involves a combination of three distinct stages: outlining the norms to be applied, giving a narrative of the case to be resolved, and applying the norms to the case in question. The normative part of casuistry focused on law as a source of obligation. The narrative part gave the important details and circumstances. And the application was a judgment of how the norms and the case in question were to be assessed. There was little difference between casuists of the eighteenth century regarding the importance of law and norms. The level of detail given in the narrative part could vary in quantity but rarely in substance. The significant difference among casuists occurs in the weighting given to norms in the final application to a moral case. These articles show how Alphonsus uses grades of probability in assessing how moral norms are to be assessed. In line with what was said in previous articles, possession is the governing concept. Freedom is the first characteristic possession of the human person for Alphonsus. Law can take its place only when it is certain and properly promulgated.

These articles should be understood as practical examples of how Alphonsus uses reflex principles when there is a difference between what the law appears to require and what the person may be free to do. This is the tension of the four situations discussed in these articles. They should be taken as illustrations of a casuistic solution to historically conditioned situations. While they illustrate that Alphonsus was not a rigorist in the application of norms, they add little to understanding how conscience is the entry point of moral theology.

ARTICLES 35-37
Possession and ownership

As with Articles 31-34, these articles are not pivotal to the purpose of this commentary. They have their own general interest for understanding Alphonsus. He was widely consulted as a lawyer because of his proficiency in contract law. His anxiety after the loss of the 1723 Amatrice legal case was life-changing, undoubtedly leading him to be even more assiduous in his examination of laws regarding ownership and possession. After the foundation of the Redemptorists, he was involved in numerous disputes about property and titles, most notably with the Sarnelli family. These articles show him to be at home in the world of contract and property law.

Their value for understanding the overall treatise on conscience is indirect. The legal argument in Articles 35-37 has an implicit structure. An owner retains the presumption to possession unless there is certainty that he has lost this right. He cannot be deprived of that right by a mere opinion. Certainty is needed. Possession is presumed, and only solid reasons (not opinions) can deprive people of their rights. With regard to implications for the treatise on conscience, there is a parallel. Possession is the presumption in law. This applies also in the law-referring moral theology of Alphonsus. Our first human possession is the freedom with which we are endowed at birth. Nothing can deprive us of that except the certainty that it has been transferred to another, and this has to be proven.

ARTICLES 38-39
Doubts about receiving Communion

The chapter closes with comments on two cases about the reception of Communion. Nothing new is added to the substance of the argument of the chapter. The difference between doubts of law and doubts of fact is again underlined, and the application of laws has to be according to the character of the particular law involved. Possession remains the central idea, as the last sentence of Article 39 confirms.

Commentary on Chapter Three, Section I

ARTICLE 40
The probable conscience

ALPHONSUS HAS ALREADY EXPLAINED WHAT HE MEANS BY CONSCIENCE: It is a practical and reasonable decision by which we judge what is good or evil in an actual situation (Article 2). It is a binding decision in the sense that acting against conscience is a sin (Article 19). What does it imply, then, to qualify the substance "conscience" with the adjective "probable"? If conscience has such an obligatory force, it must be certain; the certainty needed is adequate if it is probable. Unraveling the meaning of probable, as a qualifying adjective of conscience, is the train of thought in this chapter.

The argument is an endorsement of moral certainty as acceptable for a decision of conscience. This idea had been introduced by Jean Gerson (confer commentary on Article 19), and was revived during the theological developments of the seventeenth and eighteenth centuries. Gerson, writing at the time of the Great Western Schism, spoke of moral certainty as the necessary and accessible criterion for a serene moral and spiritual life. Alphonsus, writing during the theological disputes ignited by the issues raised by Jansenism and Laxism, applies the terminology of the probable conscience as the criterion for moral stability and spiritual progress. It is a comparable understanding of moral certainty in making a decision that links Gerson with Alphonsus.

The categories of probability that Alphonsus uses to explain his preference were part of the theological debates of his day. They are bookended in this article by the references to the propositions condemned by Pope Innocent XI in 1679 and Pope Alexander VIII in 1690. The former condemned a list of sixty-five propositions which were classified as "errors of laxist moral doctrine" and the latter condemned thirty-one "errors of the Jansenists." Both popes issued their decrees through the Holy Office and included technical references to debates that were customary in the universities, Louvain in particular. Names are mentioned. Alphonsus was aware of them, though he concentrates on pronouncements rather than personalities.

He selects two of the condemned propositions though his interest, as usual, is in practical decisions. The listing of various species of probability needs to be appreciated as part of the necessary theological program of educating priests in the eighteenth century. There are semantic difficulties in understanding the subtle differences between these brands of moral views. Whatever sense they made in the time of Alphonsus, they are now abstruse. This need not deter a contemporary reader from trying to grasp the underlying concerns. Alphonsus, in Article 40, is not preparing us to make an extrinsic moral calculus based on rarefied distinctions. The repetition of the criterion of prudence on five occasions suggests more internalized criteria; the grades of probability are not examined theoretically but in view of what a wise person should do.

Alphonsus has already shown that the distinction between the truth of something in itself *(veritas rei)* and the truth in an honest decision in practice *(veritas honestatis actionis)* is essential to his model of conscience. A person can err on the *veritas rei* but he cannot err on the *veritas honestatis actionis*. Conscience has to be followed; moral certainty is necessary for this, and the correct understanding of probability is the connection to moral certainty. Many of the different species of probability will appear again in the following section on the moral system. This will involve some comment on the complex development of the views of Alphonsus over a thirty-year period. The difficulty he tries to resolve is how an opinion (even if probable) could be part of a judgment that must be certain, because conscience is invoked.

I refer interested readers to the scholarly works of Vereecke, Capone, Majorano, Amarante, and Vidal for details on the development of the views of Alphonsus. I highlight one point. A conscience is called probable in the sense in which Alphonsus understands conscience: a practical reasonable judgment on the good to do or evil to be avoided in a particular situation. Conscience has, legitimately, other aspects that could be considered. There are varying senses of conscience, such as those outlined in the *Catechism of the Catholic Church*, 1776–1794. Alphonsus applies the criterion of probability to one of these aspects (the practical judgment), not to others. He is identifying the level of knowledge needed in order to proceed with a decision of conscience. The resignation statement of emeritus Pope Benedict XVI is an interesting example of the theology of conscience which illustrates my interpretation of Alphonsus: "Having interrogated my conscience again and again before God, I have come to the certain knowledge that, on account of my advancing years, I no longer have the strength to carry out the Petrine office." (The translation is mine, from the address given at the Consistory of February 11, 2013.)

What is good, in itself, is one question *(veritas rei)*. What is right, in practice, is another *(veritas honestatis actionis)*.

ARTICLES 41-43
Probability of fact and of law

Alphonsus returns to a distinction he already made between doubts of fact and of law (confer Article 25). I underline, once again, how the interest of Alphonsus is with the practical-existential level of a theological issue, rather than at the theoretical-essential level. The two levels are not in conflict, though the angle of a response differs, depending on which perspective the question comes from. The important distinction, for Alphonsus, is between the remote and proximate law of morality, as stated at the very beginning in Article 1. It is clear that Alphonsus considers conscience as the formally critical part of morality compared to laws, which are the material part.

Articles 41-43 explain the formal superiority of conscience with more precision. The language is straightforward, even if the basic ideas are complex. It is never lawful to use a probable view about a fact, that is, about the substance of a thing *(veritas rei)*. All the probability in the world about a reality, in this sense, cannot change its truthful status. However, it is lawful to use a probable view about the integrity of a particular action *(veritas honestatis actionis)*, because opinion is needed for the variety of elements in a moral decision. Conscience is the formal rule of morality and it must accept the material rule (law). This becomes a formal rule only through the judgment of conscience. The grades of probability given in Article 40 are the lens through which this process is verified in establishing practical certainty about the honesty and integrity of an action.

Article 43 is an interesting presentation of the difference between fact and law. Alphonsus would have learned that *facta notoria probatione non egent* (publicly known facts do not need proof) in his law studies. He had no doubt about the superiority of the Catholic religion. For him, this is a simple fact that needs no proof. It is in his dogmatic writings, such as *The Truths of the Faith* (1767) and *The History of Heresies* (1772) that his apologia for the unique truth claims of the Catholic Church are most robustly made. The freedom of religion as a fundamental right in the sense authorized by the Second Vatican Council was not part of Alphonsus' way of thinking. In this tract, he is dealing with the freedom that is conceivable, and indeed necessary, within moral choice. He is not dealing with freedom of religion as it is now typically understood. How he might have responded to this contemporary maxim can be speculated on, though we should not be distracted from the particular moral point he is making in this article. In morality, there is no replacement for the truth of a fact. However, there is a need for a solidly based opinion when one takes a moral decision in practice since this involves more than the presentation of observable factual data.

ARTICLES 44-46
Medical issues

Professionally verified standards in medical science in the eighteenth century were not common. There was a tradition of medical studies in Italian universities like Salerno, Padua, and Bologna, but few of those trained would have worked in the localities Alphonsus would have been more familiar with. Barber-surgeons, apothecaries, drug peddlers, and charlatans were accessible. These were scarcely dependable in the sense of having the sound knowledge needed for offering reliable probable opinions. In the absence of medical ethics to guide doctors or codes of ethics to oversee the profession, it is not surprising that Alphonsus deals with the question of probability in making medical decisions in a traditionally careful way within the general outlines of the Hippocratic tradition. For Alphonsus, moral medicine depended on the prudent decisions of a medical doctor.

Alphonsus insists on the safer procedures as the norm. Where there is doubt about the efficacy of a medicine, it should not be used. Decisions are to be careful and, interestingly, should include the consent of the sick person. There is such a difference between eighteenth-century Italy and technological possibilities today that it is not possible to use the categories of this article straightforwardly. There is a spirit in the approach of Alphonsus, however, that can find an echo within today's highly complex medical technology. In a message to the World Medical Association (November 17, 2017), Pope Francis suggested the criterion of "responsible closeness" as helpful in coming to proportionate decisions in end-of-life issues. There is an echo of Alphonsus in this assertion of Pope Francis.

The distinction between doubts of fact and of theory run through Articles 44-46. The primary fact is the preservation of the health of the patient, and this is to be held as sacrosanct. In particular cases, like that of seriously ill people, there will be different speculations to be taken into account when assessing which intervention to make. Using the grades of probability introduced in Article 40, one can note how Alphonsus prefers more probable or safer views in these cases. This surely reflects his respect for the integrity of the individual human life. It may also be a sign of his experience dealing with charlatans in rural areas.

The numerous references to the Salmanticenses in the notes are a sign of the esteem in which Alphonsus held this Carmelite

Cursus Theologicus. The moral commentaries were composed from 1665, and concentrated their interpretations of Aquinas' *Summa Theologiae* on practical sacramental issues. Alphonsus usually quotes this source approvingly, with some exceptions.

ARTICLE 47
Judicial decisions

Alphonsus had a finely tuned sense of the rule of law. Trained as a lawyer, he was conscious of the rule of law as the framework within which the common good was promoted. He was an innovator in terms of writing on the duties of the various personnel involved in the administration of justice (advocates, notaries, procurators, witnesses). His texts on these (*Istruzione e pratica per li confessori: Il confessore diretto per le confessioni della gente di campagna,* as well as the relevant sections of the *Theologia Moralis*) continue to be benchmarks. In Article 47, he selects the role of the judge as fundamental in explaining the proper understanding of the probable opinion. In highlighting the public role of the judge, Alphonsus is giving a significant counterpoint to the use of the probable opinion in moral decisions. The judge does not invent the law; he oversees its administration. Private opinions do not count when the facts of a legal case are to be upheld. The strong sense of the importance of equity and personal integrity in the administration of justice was already evident in the twelve rules he wrote for himself as a young advocate. They influenced his thinking, even after his legal career had finished in failure. This article, being a strong defense of the need to protect the law, is another instance of why the choice of conscience as the entry point of moral discourse is so distinctive in the theology of one who was scrupulously respectful of the law at all levels.

ARTICLES 48-51
Sacramental questions

Conscience is the entry point for all of moral theology, and this includes the understanding of the sacraments, which Alphonsus treats at length in book six of his *Theologia Moralis*. In these four articles he comments on how some of the sacraments are to be administered and received.

Alphonsus considers the sacraments as they had been explained by the Council of Trent. "They are signs instituted not by man but by God, which we firmly believe have in themselves the power of producing the sacred effects of which they are signs" (*Catechism of the Council of Trent*, 146). The fact is that they are sacred actions. In line with his view that probability can never be used to overturn the validity of an existing fact, he is definite in his exclusion of the use of the probable opinion in conferring a sacrament (Article 48). Circumstances and doubts have, as always for Alphonsus, to be considered and he deals with two of these in Articles 49 and 50. Circumstances of necessity are a matter of opinion rather than preestablished fact, and these circumstances are to be evaluated in terms of their probability (Article 49). Doubts about the jurisdictional power of the minister of the sacrament are also to be resolved in this way (Article 50). Although he allows flexibility in interpreting the situation of the person receiving the sacraments (Article 51), he urges caution because of the danger of human opinion being used to interpret what was, for him, a divine fact.

ARTICLES 52-53
An example and a conclusion

Alphonsus again uses an example to illustrate his theory. It is a simple one: A person is out hunting and is unsure whether the intended target is a human or a beast. If it is a human, in fact, then all the legal probability in the world would not bring the person back to life. Probability of fact trumps, and can never be replaced, by probability of *opinion*. However, the law is a different matter and here we are dealing with *opinions* and not simply with *facts*. Facts are facts that can be verified. Opinions are in a different category, and reaching certainty in the choice of opinion is the issue.

The maturation of Alphonsus' views is apparent in a series of published works that became the anvil on which his settled formulations depend. Three texts of Alphonsus are central to this evolution: *Dissertatio pro usu moderato opinionis probabilis* (1752), *Breve Dissertatione sull'uso moderato dell'opinione probabile* (1762), and *Dell'uso modetrato dell'opinione probabile* (1765). Referring to these titles can be confusing for someone reading the tract on conscience for the first time. It has led to different editorial choices in the presentation of the text in the editions of Heilig and Gaudé, which I referred to in the introduction. The evolution of Alphonsus' views on the use of the moderate opinion, often necessitated by the criticism of his views by other theologians (particularly Patuzzi) is beyond the scope of this commentary. I refer interested readers to the writings of Capone and Gaudé. For our purposes, it is sufficient to understand how the mature position of Alphonsus revolves around the critical difference between doubts of fact and doubts of law. In arguing that the probable opinion is sufficient for resolving doubts of law, Alphonsus is simply acknowledging that in moral matters not everything is factually predetermined.

Commentary on Chapter Three, Section II

A MORAL SYSTEM HAS A PARTICULAR MEANING FOR St. Alphonsus. It refers to the manner of using principles to resolve practical doubts of conscience. Alphonsus has already explained what he means by reflex principles (Article 26). Here, the account is expanded into a methodology through which principles, reflex and other, establish a system for resolving practical doubts of conscience. Theoretical doubts may still remain; the concern of Alphonsus is to outline a system that eliminates practical doubts.

The genealogy of moral systems has its origin in the development of moral theology after the Council of Trent (1545-1563). Before that, theology was considered as one discipline, without the divisions into dogmatic, moral, or ascetical that emerged later. There was, of course, the range of pastoral issues that constantly characterize ecclesial ministry. The classic *Summae Theologiae* did not deal with these directly and a cognate literary form grew in a parallel fashion. These were first called *Summae Confessorum* and, later, *Institutiones Morales*. The popularity of these genres owed much to their accessible style and user-friendly outline which suited a busy pastor. Though lacking in analytic thought, these *Summae* and *Institutiones* incorporated an understanding of the moral life that had theological origins. On the one hand, the habit of *synderesis* defined the capacity of the human person to perceive the major principles of the moral life (such as do good and avoid evil). On the other hand, the act of conscience defined the process of discovering the specific good to be sought or evil avoided in a particular situation. Analysis and evaluation were eventually linked through reasoning. Theology was considered a single science. These books worked within that general assumption.

Well-organized as these books were, they were limited when different issues arose because of changing times that necessitated new thinking. The most significant change was how law began to assume a dominant role in the organization of society, and eventually in theology. The collapse of the feudal system created a void, first for social cohesion and, consequently, for the theological explanation of the Christian moral life within society.

The revolutionary changes within the Western legal structure in the centuries before Alphonsus are the background to understanding why he proposed the moral system he did. The passing of medieval society, broadly a feudal way of thinking, gave rise to the need for different legal categories. As feudal law was being replaced by secular law in society, customary law was being replaced by canon law within the Church. The emergence of canon law as the first dominant modern Western legal system threw a long shadow on the development of theology. It is important to be aware of this in coming to terms with the moral system of Alphonsus. He accepted canon law as a cohesive requirement for the life of the Church. This positive acceptance was strengthened, for him, by the need to preserve the Catholic Church against inroads from the Germanic transformation of their legal system in the slipstream of the Reformation. This may seem an unnecessary historical digression when we are considering a short treatise on conscience. I make it in order to suggest a broader-than-usual understanding of why the Alphonsian emphasis on conscience has special significance.

The law, in all its forms, became the matrix of social and, subsequently, theological analysis. Law as the paradigm for theology was accepted, and the lawyer Alphonsus was at ease with it. However, the emergence of law as the theological template created novel problems for the moral life. Law, civil and ecclesiastical, sought clarity of expression, but life throws up its own dilemmas. In a situation where the law might be clear but a conscience doubtful, what is to be done? That is the precise question of the moral system of Alphonsus though it reflects, as I am suggesting, a wider-ranging social phenomenon.

The moral systems concentrated their attention on the hesitation of a conscience before an action that is not determined by law or an action that is doubtfully imposed by law. The variety of systems are set apart by the position they take on the underlying question: Is priority given to the objective law or personal liberty in reaching a decision? A number of systems emerged, reflecting distinctive preferences: tutiorism, probabiliorism, equiprobabilism, probabilism, laxism. In this complex landscape of subtly diverse shades, the principal contrast by the time of Alphonsus was provided by the Jansenists and Probabilists (often Jesuits). It was a passionate debate. The Jansenist tendency stressed what is certain through law, in order not to compromise the truth. The Probabilist tendency accommodated people who were so overtaken by difficulties that they were discouraged in the path to perfection. Paradoxically, the extremes of Jansenism and Laxism make a similar error, and were duly condemned by the Holy Office. Both were, in fact, reductionist theories. The Jansenists eliminated in practice the discernment of situations; the Laxists eliminated in practice the discernment of normative truth. This was the world of moral systems within moral theology when Alphonsus offers his own characteristic one.

ARTICLES 54-56
The fundamental principles of the system

Articles 54-56 summarize the essential principles on which the system of Alphonsus rests. The evolution of his thinking was a complex journey that took more than thirty years. I refer, again, to the studies of Vereecke, Capone, Majorano, Amarante, Vidal, and Gaudé, for those interested. My commentary is offered as an educational aid rather than attempting historical or hermeneutical analysis.

The first principle, *melior est conditio possidentis* (the position of the owner is the stronger one) is implicit in Article 54. The competing pretenders to possession are liberty and law. The word "possession" does not have much attraction for moral discourse now; it seems to belong more to the world of legal claims and disputes. That is, indeed, the background from which it comes. To understand Alphonsus' system, I suggest one understands the concept of "possession" as comparable to the fundamental quality by which a person's present status can be determined. Each of us has (possesses) characteristics by which we are generally known. In making a moral judgment, the essential question is whether we are free or not. We are free, in the moral sense used by Alphonsus, until the point when we are demonstrably no longer free. Law defines that limit. It is in this sense that *melior est conditio possidentis* (the position of the owner is the stronger one). Freedom is the basic characteristic of the human person that governs the choices made in life. Article 54 indicates that the selection of what is lawful is, however, not a simple matter of "do as you please." What is lawful in a particular action must correspond, as far as possible, to what is true. The truth of something is sought within the parameters of law (divine, natural, positive).

The second fundamental principle of the system is implicit

in Article 55: *lex dubia non obligat* (a doubtful law is not obligatory). Even if law has replaced freedom (in the sense of Article 54) there remains the question of proceeding with moral certainty. Alphonsus considers this to be so central to his system that he in effect equates a decision of moral uprightness with a decision of faith. Probability is not a slogan that justifies an argument in and by itself. The probable opinion is at the service of the prudent judgment of acting rightly according to one's conscience. So serious is the matter of acting rightly that there should be no doubt about the existence of the law if and when it replaces the original freedom of a human person.

The third fundamental principle is explicitly proposed in Article 56. Not only must doubt be eliminated, using the second principle, but it must be demonstrated that the law invoked is certain: *lex incerta non potest certam obligationem inducere* (an uncertain law cannot impose a certain obligation).

Each of the principles is important in itself and they are interlinked within a system for resolving practical doubts of conscience. In a sense, the second and third principles are more accessible to contemporary readers because they apply a legal language that is comprehensible outside moral theology. However, it is the first principle *(melior est conditio possidentis)* that sustains the theological weight of the system. During his lifetime, this principle was used in a restrictive sense, even by some probabilist theologians generally supportive of Alphonsus. Their interpretation was that the principle applied only to matters of material justice (possession of goods, in the technical sense). The insistence of Alphonsus, from the third edition of the moral theology in 1757, that the principle applies to every area of the moral life, draws attention to the characteristic theological reach of his system. Synthetically, his argument is as follows: The essence of justice is to give to each person what is his or her due; justice is the potential reason why all the other virtues are important in practice. If the law can take the place of freedom (in the sense of "possession"), it follows that the person's characteristic as a moral agent is determined by the justness of their lives.

It is occasionally claimed that Alphonsus can be a niggling legalist because he gives so much importance to law. I disagree with that interpretation, mainly because thinking theologically within legal categories was normal in his epoch. He is a casuist, certainly, but there is a theological linchpin to his system. The fundamental characteristic of the human person is the freedom granted to every person by the fact of being born human. Nothing predates that freedom, not even the law. If a point is reached in a person's life where, being rational, they confide themselves to the law of God, then the law must be as secure and guaranteed as the original freedom. Alphonsus gives ample attention to law in his moral theology, even though freedom is the original human gift. Freedom is so important that it can only be replaced by a law that is certain, known, promulgated, and applicable. Law must be as certain as freedom is, if it is to replace freedom's "possession." This needs to be proven.

The reasoning is given in the following articles. Alphonsus had been working on their formulation for a long time, as he notes multiple times. The clarity of expression is a result of theological choices that were refined in the fulcrum of debate. The precision of the final text is significant. However, it is not obvious what the text might mean for a contemporary reader. The theological choices implicit in the justification of Alphonsus of the basic principles warrant an explanation.

ARTICLE 57
Law must be promulgated

I ask readers to keep an eye to the First Corollary of the *Treatise on Conscience,* which states: *lex dubia non obligat* (a doubtful law does not oblige) from Articles 63-72. Instead of writing a separate annotation on these articles, I am incorporating what they say into my commentary on Article 57. I have judged this to be a more accessible way of familiarizing readers with the main arguments of Alphonsus on the need for law to be promulgated.

The requirement for promulgation of law is linked to a presupposition of the whole treatise; there is a distinction between the truth of something known theoretically, and the truth of honesty in a practical judgment of conscience. The former aspect of truth is determined by a direct judgment; the latter is reached through a judgment using indirect reflex principles. The essential quality of law for understanding the *Treatise on Conscience* comes from its application *(actus secundus)* rather than from its theoretic exposition *(actus primus)*. A casual reading of Alphonsus might suggest that this is not very logical, that the first should come before the second. Reading Article 71 can help the reader appreciate that there is a distinct rationality to the position of Alphonsus. I do not accept the assessment that Alphonsus is confused because, in some way, he works with a double truth, one for theory and one for practice. The truth in a practical judgment of conscience presupposes the theoretic truth, before incorporating it into practice through the use of reflex principles. It is the certainty of the principles used that gives moral certainty to the judgment reached in practice. Basic to these principles is a correct understanding of law and its promulgation.

Thomas Aquinas is quoted four times in Article 57, all being taken from the *Summa Theologiae* Ia IIae, q. 90. Interestingly, it is this question of Aquinas that is most prominent in the First Corollary as well. Alphonsus is relying on the "prince of theologians" to justify his own position. It is important to note that Alphonsus is explaining his own system and not presenting himself as an original commentator on the *Summa Theologiae*. Were his aim to have written a commentary on the text of Aquinas, he would surely have first placed question 90 in the context of the other articles in which Aquinas deals with various aspects of law (questions 90-97 discuss law according to its nature, its variety, its effects, the eternal law, the natural law, human law, law and change).

Alphonsus is interested in a particular question that arose from his experience as a missionary in the epoch when a revived jurisprudence was replacing feudal law in society and the Church: Does the law exist in this precise situation where a practical decision of conscience has to be taken? Ultimately, he concludes that the law exists only if it has been properly promulgated, and he relies on Aquinas to explain what this means. In Article 57, he does not deal with additional questions raised by Aquinas, though readers of the corollary will note how Alphonsus was familiar with other texts, including *De Veritate*. When Aquinas is writing about law, he is mindful of the dominion of law being multifaceted; law is not the exclusive preserve of theologians. When we apply a text of Aquinas on law to moral theology, it is important to remember the original context of Aquinas' own concern about law in the evaluation of moral issues. Aquinas writes about law in the moral life with an awareness of two tendencies at his own time: the potential anarchism of the Spiritualists at one extreme, the disproportionate legalism of the Penitentials at the other. No more than Alphonsus after him, Aquinas seeks a rationally convincing *via media* between extremes. However, it is not the same *via media* which Alphonsus tried to forge for practical use in a different age.

In interpreting the standard texts of Aquinas that are used in moral theology, there is no restricted explanation imposed. An interesting example in recent decades has been the debates about the encyclical letter *Veritatis Splendor* (*VS*,1993) and the post-synodal Exhortation *Amoris Laetitia* (*AL*, 2016). Both magisterial documents use some common texts from Aquinas (one of them being from question 94 of the *Summa Theologiae*, a text that was also a point of disagreement between Alphonsus and Patuzzi). There are differences of interpretation in how *Veritatis Splendor* and *Amoris Laetitia* rely on Aquinas. Does this mean that one of these magisterial texts is "wrong" and the other "right"? The context which is the background to *VS* (a magisterial preoccupation about the objective universal application of unchanging norms) and the background to *AL* (a magisterial preoccupation about the subjective application of particular norms) are different. They are not exclusive, one of the other. In an analogous sense, what Alphonsus quotes from Aquinas is an advocatory argument to justify a key part of his own moral system. Alphonsus quotes an "authority" to justify the intrinsic "reasoning" of his position. Other interpretations of Aquinas about the promulgation of law are possible. In fact, the core of the first corollary centers on how Alphonsus and G. V. Patuzzi (died 1769) interpret the same texts of Aquinas with distinctive emphases.

The practical decision of conscience is a voluntary act in the traditional vocabulary. It is a decision that has to be deliberately willed and chosen. Because of the binding force of a decision of conscience, there can be no room for doubt. Doubts may persist at the speculative level but not at the practical level. I suggest that the final paragraph of Article 65 in the First Corollary is a comprehensible explanation, by Alphonsus himself, of what he means by practical moral certainty in a decision of conscience.

How reasoning *(ratio)* can oblige the will *(voluntas)* is explained by Alphonsus in a particular way that distinguishes him from contemporaries like Patuzzi. Going through these differences of opinion, it is possible to summarize why the promulgation of the law is a prerequisite for Alphonsus. A person cannot be obliged to do something unless he is certain that he is bound to do it (confer Article 68). The only way in which a person can know that he is bound to do something is when he knows the law obliges him (confer Article 69). People must know this, not simply have some vague opinion about it. This certain knowledge of a properly promulgated law applies to all levels of law: human law (confer Article 69), divine law (confer Article 70), and natural law (confer Article 71). I offer a short comment on Alphonsus' position on each of these levels of law.

On human law, Alphonsus insists that the level of promulgation necessary is within the conscience of a person. It is not enough that there has been material promulgation or general notification that such-and-such has been decreed by some authority. The person who has a practical decision to make must actually know, in conscience, that there is a human law relevant to the decision.

The divine law exists from eternity. But what does this mean, in practice, for conscience? Alphonsus is circumspect. Though it exists from eternity, does the divine law exist precisely as law? God can promulgate the law to himself (or can he?). The exchange of Alphonsus with Patuzzi on this question reveals that Alphonsus was wary of a literal interpretation of the divine law. While retaining the deference one expects from a saint and doctor of the Church with regard to divine law, he does not overstretch the implications because of his conviction that law obliges only when it is promulgated in the conscience of the person.

It is in the comments on law of nature that the theological choices of Alphonsus are most clear. There is a law of nature, but it can be called law only when a person becomes aware of it (generally, around the age of reason, which modern scholars still put at six to seven years). Alphonsus is very clear on this, particularly in the final paragraphs of Article 71. It is possible to be ignorant of the law of nature in practice even if, in theory, this does not seem thinkable. Reading the comments of Alphonsus on the law of nature, it is important not to allow modern debates to deflect from the text of Alphonsus. For him, the concept of natural law as participation in the divine law is automatic. For our generation, there is a different, legitimate, and necessary debate about the meaning of the law of nature, given what we now know (or don't know) about nature.

The text of Alphonsus will not be a primary contributor to the contemporary debate on the scientific meaning of the law of nature. What can be excluded from these debates, however, on the basis of the text of Alphonsus, is a reductionist view of nature. The only acceptable view of the law of nature is that it is a law of *reason* which must be *known*. A biological reductionism of nature is not compatible with the text of Alphonsus. He makes a significant point in his comments on Patuzzi in Article 71. There is a difference between the material and formal senses of law. In the material sense, law can be a sort of habit; in the formal sense, law is a type of action. It is action that is the focus of the attention of Alphonsus. The law of nature operates in the theology of Alphonsus in the sense that it is a *lumen* (light) that one presumes is present to post-age-of-reason people. The presumption may not, always be correct.

The promulgation of law is pivotal to the understanding of Alphonsus in a decision of conscience. I give his position in a summary point-by-point form. Law, not sufficiently promulgated, leaves a person in the state of freedom into which he is born. A law that is not properly promulgated can have no effect on the liberty of a person. A law that is not properly promulgated can only create uncertainty. One cannot act with uncertainty in practice. In order to say that the law takes the place of freedom in a person's conscience, the strict criteria of promulgation must be satisfied, whether the law be the eternal, human, or natural.

The argument of this Article 57 (and the First Corollary) is, in the main, an intrinsic one. Authors are quoted (principally Aquinas), but the inherent aspect of the argument of Alphonsus is striking. Among the other authors quoted, there are a number of patristic ones (for example, in Article 66). Worthy of notice, again, are the number of quotations from Jean Gerson (for example, in Articles 67 and 71) as the most important exponent of moral certainty in medieval times. As is often the case with Alphonsus, he uses an example to show how his system works in practice (as in Article 72).

ARTICLES 58-60
Law must be certain before it can impose an obligation that is certain

Articles 58-60 are also significant for understanding the moral system of Alphonsus. Law, to impose an obligation, must not only be promulgated. It must be promulgated as a law that is certain.

There are two intertwining threads to the argument. The first is a continuation of the premise stated in Article 1: human actions are governed by the remote rule of the divine law and the proximate rule of conscience. Alphonsus is concerned, theologically, with the formal rule of conscience. He returns consistently to what is to be considered as a certain obligation in conscience. Conscience is a practical judgment by which we decide what is right or wrong in a particular situation, as outlined in Article 2.

For Alphonsus, problems of conscience are within the context of pastoral ministry; peace of conscience is guaranteed only by certainty in conscience.

The second thread is the theological justification of this position as to when and how we know that a law is certain. Alphonsus had come under increasing attack from other, mainly Dominican, theologians who regarded his approach as laxist. Alphonsus takes care to show that his views are not too accommodating; they are solid and acceptable because they are based on the text of Thomas Aquinas.

In commenting on these articles, I will be referring to the Second Corollary, Articles 73-83. The title to this corollary, "An uncertain law cannot lead to a certain obligation, because the liberty of a person is in possession prior to laws" is the warp into which the threads of Alphonsus' moral system are woven.

The defense of the elemental freedom of the human person is the defining trait of the Alphonsian system of moral theology. So important is this freedom that it cannot be substituted by anything that is less certain than freedom itself. The attention which Alphonsus gives to law, its promulgation and certainty, is understandable only when one appreciates the place of freedom in his system. He defends this position in a step-by-step way that reflects a clarity that was polished only after serious engagement in debate.

His basis is uncomplicated. Because the law is the way of measuring something, one must know the law by which an action is measured. He accepts the difficulty in this assertion, particularly as regards to divine law. Article 73 takes up this challenge. The divine law exists in the mind of God, but not necessarily in the human mind. However, if law is to be used by humans, it has to be certain as a law. Alphonsus relies on a text of Aquinas (*De Veritate*, question 17, article 3) to explain that the certainty of a law must be a certainty that is found in the conscience of the person making the decision. This dilemma emerged in the pastoral ministry of Alphonsus. His reliance on Thomas Aquinas, evident throughout these articles, is to demonstrate that his position is consonant with Aquinas, acknowledged by all as the master theologian. Not everyone agreed with the interpretation of Alphonsus, particularly the already mentioned Patuzzi. These exchanges did not reconcile their position. I comment on them by considering the major objections which Patuzzi made to Alphonsus, and how Alphonsus responded. It is important, again, to realize that Alphonsus is not engaging in a scholastic debate to show who is the better interpreter of Thomas. The interest of Alphonsus is a different one. He knows what the practical problems of conscience are and he proposes a system to deal with these. He is now demonstrating that his views are compatible with texts from Aquinas.

The texts that are the focus of the objections of Patuzzi are *De Veritate*, question 17 and *De Malo*, question 3. For Patuzzi, knowledge is sufficient if there is a general notification of something. Alphonsus rejects this material understanding of knowledge as too restrictive; knowledge has to be located in the conscience of the person. General notification is not enough. Alphonsus chides Patuzzi that he is not up to date on how modern dictionaries explain "notification" (Article 74). Compressing Alphonsus in simple terms, he argues that you can only sin if you know you are sinning. The material knowledge of something is never enough to ground the formal decision that is involved in conscience. Alphonsus is explicit on this point in Article 58 when he quotes Gonet (1616-1681):

> Quite often it is a matter of chance, and not of the will, that a person sins or does not sin, in that it seems that

what he does is in conformity or not with the natural law of which he is ignorant. This is indeed an absurd position, since the true and only cause of sin is the will which acts in a way that is not in conformity with the rules of morals.

The fact that he can quote a Dominican in his favor would not have been lost on Patuzzi.

The necessity for knowledge is strengthened by the position of Alphonsus on the precedence of freedom in God's design.

> Thus, by the priority of reason, the human person was first considered by God as free, and only then was consideration given to a law by which the human could be bound. To take an example: from eternity, God prohibited murder, therefore by the priority of reason he first considered people who were capable of murder, and afterward he gave the precept that one should not kill another person (Article 75).

The precedence of freedom in the system of Alphonsus is not an abstract affirmation. Typically, he applies what he says to practice: "where the law is unclear, and to support it there is no clear scriptural text, or decision by the church, or clear argument, then nothing should be condemned as a grave sin." The objections which Patuzzi made to Alphonsus were those of a theorist who feared that the promotion of freedom would lead to general moral depravity. Alphonsus was surely no libertine, but he rejects the rigorist position as going against the design of God:

> Therefore, the principle of our adversaries is a false one that, in doubt the law is in possession and, accordingly, the safer position is to be taken in a doubt. But Fr. Patuzzi

says: "if liberty is in possession why does St. Thomas write that, in doubt, following the more benign opinion does not excuse from everything?" It is to be answered that the holy doctor is here not talking about the final practical judgment (Article 75).

The system of Alphonsus can be understood by accepting his insistence that conscience is a practical judgment. The difference with Patuzzi on the interpretation of Thomas Aquinas is, in the final analysis, a difference of opinion about pastoral prudence rather than textual analysis. Article 80 explains the theology of Alphonsus on sin in terms of the difference between breaking a law in a material sense and sinning in the formal sense:

> The person who uses an equally probable opinion, basing himself on a certain principle, is a person in danger of transgressing the law but not of sinning...it is necessary to distinguish a certain law from an uncertain one (Article 80).

Writing, as he does, for prospective pastoral ministers, Alphonsus takes care to show how the certainty needed for a law to oblige involves an appropriate relationship between knowledge of the law and the experience of freedom. I consider Article 76 to be an important link in understanding why an uncertain law cannot impose a certain obligation in the moral life of a Christian. In this article, Alphonsus is responding to the third objection of Patuzzi that "nothing is allowed to us except what is in conformity to the divine will. I am happy that they make this objection to me, because on this point St. Thomas teaches all that is sufficient to entirely uphold our opinion...." The article hinges on a significant number of quotations from Aquinas' *Prima Ia Iae, IIa IIae* and *De Veritate.*

The critical distinction, for Alphonsus, is the obedience given to God as God, and the obedience given to God as known to the person. Unless the person really knows that this is actually the will of God, then calling it the will of God is pointless. Alphonsus is correctly known, especially through his spiritual writings, for insisting that we follow the will of God in all things. His short treatise *On Conformity to the Will of God,* first published in 1755, is considered a classic of its genre. The moral steps involved in actually knowing the will of God is what becomes clearer from Article 76. The negative formulation in Article 76 ("the divine will does not oblige unless there is knowledge of it, unless this knowledge is most certain, unless this knowledge is scientific and unless that knowledge is made manifest") should be understood as a positive invitation to seek God's will as it is known to the conscience. It is our will which should conform to God's will. We will everything that is good, in a general sense, but in a particular situation we are not to presume we know God's will without taking the steps to prepare us for that.

These significant articles are dependent on texts from Aquinas. Other theologians are quoted, particularly in Article 60. They are ancillary to the basic texts of Aquinas. I would note, however, the references to two particular authors. Gerson is quoted in all three articles: the major protagonist for the theory of moral certainty is taken by Alphonsus as a sure authority on this topic. The positive citation from his contemporary Eusebius Amort (1692-1775) in Article 60 is a sign of how Alphonsus kept up to date, not only to refute Patuzzi, but to clarify an argument.

ARTICLES 61-63
Final comments

Alphonsus rests his case. The opening paragraph of Article 61 summarizes his argument. Law must be properly promulgated and certainly known before it can impose an obligation that is certain. Basing himself on Thomas Aquinas (again) he takes as sufficiently proven that an uncertain law cannot impose a certain obligation.

But there is still something to be added in view of what others have been writing against his opinions. This is dealt with in the rest of Article 61 and the following articles. Alphonsus has centered his argument on the proper use of the probable opinion. What happens, however, if there are two equally probable opinions?

An important point to note is that Alphonsus is talking about probability between two (and only two) options: the opinion in favor of freedom, and the opinion in favor of law. The equiprobability referred to is the probability of freedom *or* of law. He is not writing about equiprobability *within* freedom or the law.

A second aspect to bear in mind is that, though the concept of equiprobability is familiar within mathematical sciences (such as the quantum theory) and the social sciences (as with statistical probability theories in predicting outcomes), its use in Alphonsus is more restricted and historically conditioned. The treatise on conscience is a defense of his system of moral theology for guaranteeing certainty of conscience in practical moral decisions. The fundamental certainty for Alphonsus is the gift of freedom given to each human person at birth. This freedom can only be replaced by a certainty of law that is sufficiently solid to take the place of the original freedom. The probable opinion can be the basis for a practical judgment that is certain. Some began to ask whether two opinions could be equally probable. The spark that lit this

theological fire was a decree of the Holy Office (1680) on probabilism and probabiliorism which seemed to restrict members of the
Society of Jesus in their use of the probable opinion. The debate
is technical, and is now of mainly historical interest. To sense
the depth of controversy in the time of Alphonsus, it is useful to
recall that probabilism was associated with laxism. Those of more
rigorist views argued that it needed to be vigorously rejected
by using a safer theory of morality. The safer view, *de facto*, was
presumed to be the only solidly based option. Alphonsus opposed
this position in theory (as these articles demonstrate) though it
was the practical consequences of any theory that counted most
with him. Article 83 spells this out:

> So much for the theory. But in so far as it touches on the
> practice of choosing opinions, it is common to ask: Is it
> expedient to prefer the rigid or the benign opinion? Here
> is my answer. When it is a question of removing a peni-
> tent from the danger of formal sin, the confessor, general-
> ly speaking and in so far as Christian prudence suggests,
> uses the benign opinion. Where, in truth, the benign
> opinions bring back the danger of formal sin...the confes-
> sor...is bound to use the more safe opinions...but I do not
> know in what way it can be taught with a good conscience
> (generally speaking) that penitents who, on the basis of
> completing the confession of their guilt, were ready at
> that moment to have a certain right to absolution, that it
> can now be denied to them, because the penitent caught
> between two opinions, does not wish to follow the safer
> one. This is the type of rigidity which I consider and re-
> gard without doubt to be immoderate and unjust, since
> this type of austerity could be the cause that many souls
> are damned.

Three points in Article 63 give an indication of the theological thinking of Alphonsus. The first is the reference to Flavianus Ricci. He was a contemporary of Alphonsus, and it would seem they were familiar with each other. Alphonsus, untypically, uses his baptismal name in the fourth paragraph. Ricci had published an edition of a moral theology of the Franciscan Anacletus Reiffenstuel (1641–1703) which was widely used. Thirty different editions can be traced. Flavianus Ricci edited one of these in the 1750s. Alphonsus took issue with the fact that Ricci imposed a more rigorous interpretation on the text of Anacletus who was generally of the probabilist school favored by Alphonsus. Ricci extended the promulgation of the divine law from the general to the particular in a way that made freedom doubtful (Article 63, first paragraph).

A second glimpse into the mind of Alphonsus is his reference to his own *Dissertation on the Moderate Use of the Probable Opinion* (1755). There is more to be read about his opinions than can be presented in a handbook for students.

His comment, in the final paragraph, on the interpretation of Ecclesiasticus "he who loves danger will live by the danger" may surprise those who imagine Alphonsus as using Scripture in a proof-text way. The context of Scripture must be first deciphered.

The text ends (as it had begun in the opening articles) by recalling that the moral system rests on the views of Thomas Aquinas. The original gift of God is our freedom. Life will bring its own doubts, and we may need to have recourse to law to solve them. These practical doubts must be solved in a way that gives certainty to the practical judgment of conscience.

Endnotes

Chapter One: The Meaning of Conscience

1. Thomas Aquinas (1225-1274), *Summa Theologiae*, Ia IIae, q. 19, art. 4, corp.
2. Thomas Aquinas (1225-1274), *Quaestiones Quodlibetales*, 3, art. 27, corp.
3. Thomas Aquinas (1225-1274), *Summa Theologiae*, Ia, q. 79, art. 12, corp.
4. Letter to the Romans, 14:13.
5. G. Estius (1542-1613), *In Epistolam ad Romanos*.
6. Pope Innocent III (1161-1216, Pope from 1198 until death), *Litteras 13, de Restitutione Spoliatorum*.
7. Antoninus of Florence, (1365-1459), *Summa Theologica*.
8. Martin Navarrus de Azpilcueta (1491-1586), *Manuale Praeludium*.
9. F. Suarez (1548-1617), *De Voluntario et Involuntario*.
10. Thomas Aquinas (1225-1274), *De Veritate*, q. 15, art. 4, ad 10.
11. Salmanticenses, *Cursus Theologicus Complectens Summam Theologicam S. Thomae* and *Cursus Theologicus Moralis*, Venice 1708-1717. Throughout, I give general references to these works. The notes in the Gaudé edition normally give a precise reference, and digital searches are recommended as a follow-up to these.
12. Ferdinand Castropalaus (1581-1633), *Opus Morale*.
13. J. Azor (1535-1608), *Institutiones Theologiae Moralis*.
14. F. Suarez (1548-1617), *De Censuris*.
15. G. Vasquez (1549-1604), *In Primam Secundae*.
16. M. Bonacina (1585-1631), *Opera de Morali Theologia*.
17. M. Wigandt (died 1708), *Tribunale Confessariorum et Ordinandorum*.
18. F. Cuniliati (1685-1759), *De Conscientia*.
19. A. Franzoja (died 1760), *Theologia Morum ab Hermann Busenbaum tradita*.
20. Thomas Aquinas (1225-1274), *Summa Theologiae*, Ia IIae, q. 19, art. 6, ad 1.
21. Thomas Aquinas (1225-1274), *Quaestiones Quodlibetales*, 3, art. 27.
22. D. Concina (1687-1756), *Theologia Christiana Dogmatico-Moralis et Apparatus ad eamdem*.

23. Ibid.

24. Bernard of Clairvaux (1090-1153), *Liber de Praecepto et Dispensationibus*.

25. T. Sanchez (1550-1610), *Opus Morale in Praecepta Decalogi*.

26. J. Granado (1572-1632), *Commentarium in Summam Theologiae S. Thomae*.

27. Natalis Alexander (1639-1724), *Theologia Dogmatica et Moralis secundum ordinem Catechismi Concilii Tridentini*.

28. J. Gerson (1363-1429), *De Praeparatione ad Missam et pollutione nocturna*.

29. Antoninus of Florence (1389-1459), *Summa Theologica*.

30. Ibid.

31. J. F. Bacci (an Oratorian of the seventeenth century), *Vita di San Filippo Neri* (first edition 1622).

32. Francis de Sales (1567-1622), *Introductio ad Vitam Devotam*.

33. Glossa, In cap. *Ad aures, de tempor. Ordinationis* v. *Obedientiam*.

34. Bernard of Clairvaux (1090-1153), *Liber De Praecepto et Dispensatione*.

35. Ignatius of Loyola (1491-1556), *Epistolae Praepositorum Generalium (etiam S. Ignatii) ad Patres et Fratres SJ*.

36. Humbert of the Romans (circa 1195-1277), *Speculum Religiosorum*.

37. Denis the Carthusian (1402-1471), *In Libros Quattuor Sententiarum*.

38. Bonaventure of Umbria (1221-1274), *Speculum Discipuli*.

39. D. Concina (1687-1756), *Compendium Theologicum*.

40. J. Alvarez (1560-1620), *Opera Spiritualia*.

41. J. Azor (1535-1603), *Institutiones Theologiae Moralis*.

42. M. Bonacina (circa 1585-1631), *Opera de Morali Theologia*.

43. M. Becanus (1563-1624), *Summa Theologiae Scholasticae*.

44. A. Coninck (1571-1633), *De Sacramentis et Censuris*.

45. P. Laymann (1575-1635), *Theologia Moralis*.

46. M. Wigandt (circa 1640-1708), *Tribunale Confessariorum et Ordinandoroum*.

47. T. Sanchez (1550-1610), *Opus Morale in Praecepta Decalogi*.

48. Antoninus of Florence (1389-1459), *Summa Theologica*.

49. J. Gerson (1363-1429*), De Praeparatione ad Missam et pollutione nocturna*.

50. G. Valentia (1551-1603), *Commentarii Theologici in Summam Divi Thomae*.

51. A. Corduba (1485-1578), *Quaestionarium Theologicum*.

52. Salmanticenses, confer ch.1, note 11.

53. Cajetan [Thomas de Vio] (1469-1534), *Commentarii in Summam Theologicam*.

54. M. Navarrus (1491-1586), *Opera*.

55. F. Castropalaus (1581-1633), *Opus Morale*.

56. M. Bonacina (circa 1585-1631), *Opera de Morali Theologia*.

57. V. Filliuccius (1566-1622), *Quaestionum Moralium*.

58. D. Concina (1687-1756), *Theologia Christiana, Dogmatico-Moralis, et Apparatus ad eamdem*.

59. C. Roncaglia (1677-1737), *Universa Moralis Theologia*.

60. R. Anacletus (1641-1703), *Theologia Moralis*.

61. Salmanticenses, confer ch.1, note 11.

62. D. Concina (1687-1756), *Theologia Christiana Dogmatico-Moralis et Apparatus ad eamdem*.

63. J. Gerson (1363-1429), *Tractatus de Conscientia et Scrupulis*.

64. Ibid.

Chapter Two: The Indecisive Conscience

65. G. Vasquez (1551-1604), *Commentarium et Disputationes in D. Thomam*.

66. T. Sanchez (1550-1610), *Opus Morale in Praecepta Decalogi*.

67. J. Azor (1535-1603), *Institutiones Morales*.

68. M. Bonacina (circa 1585-1631), *Opera de Morali Theologia*.

69. F. Castropalaus (1581-1633), *Opus Morale*.

70. M. Navarrus (1493-1587), *Consilia et Responsa*.

71. G. Valentia (1551-1603), *Commentarii Theologici in Summam D. Thomae*.

72. G. Granado (1572-1632), *Commentarium in Summam Theologiae S. Thomae*.

73. Continuator Tournely [P. Collet] (1693-1770), *Universa Moralis Theologia*.

74. Augustine of Hippo (354-430), *Contra Faustum*. Article 66 of the First Corollary takes up this question.

75. Thomas Aquinas (1225-1274), *In Quattuor Libros Sententiarum*, Dist. 15, q. 2, art. 4, sol 2.

76. J. Cabassutius (1605-1685), *Theoria et Praxis Iuris Canonici*.

77. F. Suarez (1548-1617), *De Religione*.

78. T. Sanchez (1550-1610), *Opus morale in Praecepta Decalogi*.

79. R. Anacletus (1641-1703), *Theologia Moralis*.

80. Salmanticenses, confer ch. 1, note 11.

81. C. Roncaglia (1677-1737), *Universa Theologia Moralis*.

82. Salmanticenses, confer ch. 1, note 11.

83. F. de Lugo (1590-1652), *Tractatus de Septem Sacramentis*.

84. D. Concina (1687-1756), *Theologia Christiana*.

85. P. Antoine (1678-1743), *Theologia Moralis Universa*.

86. V. Filliuccius (1566-1622), *Quaestionum Moralium*.

87. P. Leander (1591-1663), *Quaestiones Morales Theologicae*.

88. F. Suarez (1548-1617), *De Religione*.

89. P. Laymann (1575-1635), *Theologia Moralis*.

90. T. Sanchez (1550-1610), *Opus Morale in Praecepta Decalogi*.

91. M. Bonacina (1585-1631), *Opera de Morali Theologia*.

92. J. Azor (1535-1603), *Institutiones Morales*.

93. T. Cajetan (1469-1564), *Commentarii in Summam Theologicam S. Thomae*.

94. Continuator Tournely [Peter Collet] (1693-1770), *Universa Moralis Theologia*.

95. Antoninus of Florence (1399-1459), *Summa Theologica*.

96. Bonaventure of Umbria (1221-1274), *Opera Omnia*.

97. Continuator Tournely, [Peter Collet] (1693-1770), *Universa Moralis Theologia*.

98. L. Lessius (1554-1623), *De Iustitia et Iure*.

99. T. Sanchez (1550-1610), *Opus Morale in Praecepta Decalogi*.

100. P. Laymann (1575-1635), *Theologia Moralis*.

101. T. Sanchez (1550-1610), *Opus Morale in Praecepta Decalogi*.

102. H. Busenbaum (1609-1668), *Medulla Theologiae Moralis*.

103. D. Soto (1494-1560), *De Iustitia et Iure*.

104. L. Habert (1635-1718), *Theologia Dogmatica et Moralis*.

105. M. Wigandt (died 1708), *Tribunale Confessariorum et Ordinandorum*.

106. C. Roncaglia (1677-1737), *Universa Moralis Theologia*.

107. T. Sanchez (1550-1610), *Opus Morale in Precepta Decalogi*.

108. Salmanticenses, confer ch. 1, note 11.

109. T. Sanchez (1550-1610), *Opus Morale in Praecepta Decalogi*.

110. P. Laymann (1575-1635), *Theologia Moralis*.

111. A. Diana (1585-1663), *Resolutiones Morales*.

112. P. Sporer (circa 1620-1683), *Theologia Moralis Decalogalis et Sacramentalis*.

113. A. Coninck (1571-1633), *Commentarii ac Disputationes in Universam Doctrinam S. Thomae de Sacramentis et Censuris*.

114. G. Valentia (1551-1603), *Commentarii Theologici in Summam D. Thomae*.

115. Salmanticenses, confer ch. 1, note 11.

116. F. Castropalaus (1581-1633), *Opus Morale*.

117. F. de Lugo, (1580-1652), *De Justitia et Iure*.

118. C. Lacroix (1652-1714), *Theologia Moralis*.

119. N. Mazzotta (died 1746), *Theologia Moralis*.

120. P. Sporer, (circa 1620-1683), *Theologia Moralis*.

121. Augustine of Hippo (354-430), *De Fide et Operibus*.

122. T. Sanchez (1550-1610), *Opus Morale in Praecepta Decalogi*.

123. C. Sfondratus (1644-1696), *Regale Sacerdotium*.

124. C. Roncaglia (1677-1737), *Universa Moralis Theologia.*

125. M. Renzi (fl. 1670), *Encyclopedia Universae Theologiae Moralis.*

126. A. Tamburini (1591-1675), *De Jure et Privilegiis Abbatum.*

127. D. Viva (1648-1710), *Opusculum de Conscientia Dubia.*

128. J. Salas (1553-1612), *Disputationes in Iam IIae Divi Thomae.*

129. C. Lacroix (1652-1714), *Theologia Moralis.*

130. D. Viva (1648-1710), *Cursus Theologiae Moralis.*

131. M. Wigandt (died 1708), *Tribunale Confessariorum et ordinandorum.*

132. F. de Lugo (1590-1652), *De Iustitia et Iure.*

133. C. Lacroix (1652-1714), *Theologia Moralis.*

134. Ibid.

135. C. Roncaglia (1677-1737), *Universa Moralis Theologia.*

136. Salmanticenses, confer ch. 1, note 11.

137. F. Castropalaus (died 1633), *Opus Morale.*

138. M. Bonacina (died 1631), *Opera de morali theologia.*

139. A. Tamburini (1591-1675), *Theologia Moralis.*

140. H. Villalobos (died 1637), *Summa de la Teologia Moral y Canonical.*

141. C. Lacroix (1562-1714), *Theologia Moralis.*

142. C. Roncaglia (1677-1737), *Universa Moralis Theologia.*

143. Ibid.

144. Salmanticenses, confer ch. 1, note 11.

145. F. de Lugo (1580-1652), *Tractatus de Septem Sacramentis.*

146. P. Laymann (1575-1635), *Theologia Moralis.*

147. A. Diana (1585-1663), *Resolutiones Morales.*

148. C. Lacroix, (1652-1714), *Theologia Moralis.*

149. H. Busenbaum (1609-1668), *Medulla Theologiae Moralis.*

150. P. Sporer (died 1683), *De Sacramentis.*

151. F. de Lugo (1580-1652), *De Septem Sacramentis.*

152. Synod of Braga (Portugal), 561-574.

153. Council of Toledo (Spain), 485-486.

154. Council of Constance (Switzerland), 1414-1418.

155. F. de Lugo (1580-1652), *Tractatus de Septem Sacramentis.*

156. Ibid.

157. E. Amort (1692-1775), *Theologia Eclectica Moralis et Scholastica.*

Chapter Three, Section I: The Probable Conscience

158. Pope Innocent XI (1611-1689: Pope from 1676 until death), *Propositiones LXV Damnatae in Decreto S. Officii 2 Mart. 1679.* Text in H. Denzinger, *Enchiridion Symbolorum Definitionum et Declarationum de rebus Fidei et Morum,* 2103.

159. Pope Alexander VIII (1610-1691, Pope from 1689 until death), *Decretum Sancti Officii 7 Dec. 1690. Errores Jansenistarum.* Text in H. Denzinger, *Enchiridion Symbolorum Definitionum et Declarationum de rebus Fidei et Morum,* 2303.

160. Salmanticenses, confer ch. 1, note 11.

161. Ibid.

162. Ibid.

163. Ibid.

164. T. Sanchez (1550-1610), *Opus Morale in Praecepta Decalogi.*

165. Salmanticenses, confer ch. 1, note 11.

166. Ibid.

167. T. Sanchez (1550-1610), *Opus Morale in Praecepta Decalogi.*

168. H. Busenbaum (1609-1668), *Medulla theologiae moralis.*

169. V. Filliuccius (1566-1622), *Quaestionum Moralium.*

170. Salmanticenses, confer ch. 1, note 11.

171. P. Antoine (1678-1743), *Theologia Moralis Universa.*

172. Pope Innocent XI (1611-1689, Pope from 1676 until death), *Propositiones LXV Damnatae in Decreto S. Officii 2 Mart. 1679.* Text in H. Denzinger, *Enchiridion Symbolorum Definitionum et Declarationum de Rebus Fidei et Morum,* 2102.

173. J. Cardenas (1613-1684), *Crisis Theologica Bipartita sive Disputationes Selectae.*

174. Pope Innocent XI (1611-1689, Pope from 1676 until death), *Propositiones LXV Damnatae in Decreto S. Officii 2 Mart. 1679.* Test in H. Denzinger, *Enchiridion Symbolorum Definitionum et Declarationum de rebus Fidei et Morum,* 2101.

175. A. Holzmann (died 1748), *Theologia Moralis.*

176. P. Antoine (1678-1743), *Theologia Moralis Universa.*

177. F. Cuniliati (1685-1759), *Universa Theologia Moralis Accurata Complexio.*

178. C. Lacroix (1652-1714), *Theologia Moralis.*

179. P. Sporer (died 1683), *Theologia Moralis.*

180. F. de Lugo (1580-1652), *Tractatus de Septem Sacramentis.*

181. J. Cardenas (1613-1684), *Crisis Theologica, sive Disputationes Selectae ex Morali Theologica.*

182. J. Cardenas, ibid.

183. A. Viva (1648-1710), *Cursus Theologiae Moralis.*

184. J. Lacroix (1652-1714), *Theologia Moralis.*

Chapter Three, Section II: The Moral System

185. Thomas Aquinas (1225-1274), *De Veritate*, q. 17, art. 3, sed contra.

186. C. Lupus (1612-1681), *Dissertatio de Usu Sententiae Probabili.*

187. Thomas Aquinas (1225-1274), *Summa Theologiae*, Ia IIae, q. 90, art. 1.

188. Ibid., art. 4.

189. *Decretum Gratiani*, twelfth century.

190. Thomas Aquinas (1225-1274), *Summa Theologiae*, Ia IIae, q. 90, art. 4.

191. F. Henno (fl. 1708-1718), *Theologia Dogmatica ac Scholastica.*

192. L. Habert (1635-1718), *Tractatus de Legibus.*

193. V. Gotti (1664-1742), *Theologia Scholastico-dogmatica.*

194. D. Soto (1494-1560), *De Iustitia et Iure.*

195. A. Duvallius (1564-1638), *Commentarium in Ia IIae.*

196. J. Gonet (1616-1681), *Clypeus Theologiae Thomisticae.*

197. J. Lorichius (1540-1610), *Thesaurus Novus Utriusque Theologiae Theoreticae et Practicae.*

198. J. Patutius (1700-1769), *Ethica Christiana sive Theologia Moralis.*

199. Thomas Aquinas (1225-1274), *Summa Theologiae*, Ia IIae, q. 90, art. 4 ad 1um.

200. F. Silvius (1581-1649), *Commentarii in Summam Sancti Thomae,* In Ia IIae, q. 90, art. 4 ad 1um.

201. John Gerson (1363-1429), *De Vita Spirituali Animae.*

202. P. de Lorca (1554-1606), *Commentarii et Disputationes in Universam Ia IIae Sancti Thomae.*

203. Can. *Erit autem.*

204. Thomas Aquinas (1225-1274), *Summa Theologiae,* Ia Iae, q. 19, art. 4, ad 3.

205. Ibid.

206. P. Collet (1693-1770), *Institutiones Theologicae.*

207. John Gerson (1363-1429), *De Vita Spirituali Animae.*

208. J. Gonet (1616-1681), *Clypeus Theologicae Thomisticae.*

209. Ibid.

210. F. Silvius (1581-1649), *Commentarii in Summam Sancti Thomae et Opuscula.*

211. F. Cuniliati (1685-1759), *Theologia Moralis.*

212. J. Lorichius (1540-1612), *Thesaurus Novus.*

213. Thomas Aquinas (1225-1274), *De Veritate,* q. 17, art. 3, in corpore.

214. Ibid.

215. Ibid.

216. Thomas Aquinas (1225-1274), *Summa Theologiae,* Ia IIae q. 90, art. 1, in corpore.

217. Thomas Aquinas (1225-1274), *Summa Theologiae,* Ia IIae q. 19, art. 10, pr.

218. Thomas Aquinas, (1225-1274), *Summa Theologiae,* Ia IIae q. 19, art. 10, ad 1.

219. Thomas Aquinas, (1225-1274), *Summa Theologiae,* Ia IIae q. 19, art. 10, resp. ad 1.

220. J. Gonet (1616-1681), *Clypeus Theologicae Thomisticae.*

221. J. Gerson (1363-1429), *De Vita Spirituali Animae.*

222. Thomas Aquinas (1225-1274), *Summa Theologiae,* IIa, IIae, q. 104, art. 4.

223. Thomas Aquinas (1225-1274), *Summa Theologiae,* IIa, IIae, q. 104, art. 4, ad 3.

224. T. Raymond (1582-1663), *De Paenitentia, Liber 3.*

225. Lactantius (circa 250-circa 325), *Opera. Institutiones,* in Migne, Patrologia Latina, Volumes 6 and 7.

226. J. Nider (circa 1380-1438), *Consolatorium Timoratae Conscientiae.*

227. Antoninus of Florence (1389-1459), *Summa Theologica.*

228. G. Biel (1420-1495), *Collectoria super 4 Libros Sententiarum.*

229. D. Soto (1494-1560), *De Iustitia et Jure.*

230. Ibid.

231. P. Lambertini (1675-1758, Pope Benedict XIV, 1740 until death), *Raccolta di alcuni Notificazioni, editi ed Istruzioni.*

232. M. Cano (1509-1560), *Praelectiones de Poenitentia.*

233. J. Rocafull, (fl. 1648), *Praxis Totius Theologiae Moralis.*

234. F. Suarez (1548-1617), *De Censuris.*

235. J. Ildephonsus (fl. 1628), *Commentaria in Ia IIae Sancti Thomae.*

236. E. Amort (1692-1775), *Theologia Eclectica Moralis et Scholastica.*

237. Ibid.

238. G. Vasquez (1551-1604), *Commentarium et Disputationes in D. Thomam et Opuscula Moralia.*

239. J. de Lugo (1583-1660), *Disputationes Scholasticae et Morales.*

240. B. Mastrius (1602-1673), *Disputationes Theologicae in 4 Libros Sententiarum.*

241. A. Holzmann (died 1748), *Theologia Moralis.*

242. C. Roncaglia (1677-1737), *Universa Moralis Theologia.*

243. Salmanticenses, confer ch. 1, note 11.

244. J. Heinneccius (1681-1741), *Opera ad Universam Iurisprudentiam, Philosophiam et Literas Humaniores Pertinentia.*

245. *Institutiones de Iure Personarum.*

246. *Cum in Iure, de Officio et Potestate Judicis Delegati.*

247. Thomas Aquinas (1225-1274), *In 4 Sententiarum,* Dist. 15, q. 2, art. 4, ad 2.

248. Ibid.

249. F. Ricci (fl. 1770), *Anacleti Reiffenstuel Theologia Moralis Instaurata.*

250. Thomas Aquinas (1225-1274), *De Veritate*, q. 17, art. 3.

251. Thomas Aquinas (1225-1274), *Summa Theologiae*, Ia IIae q. 90, art. 1.

252. V. L. Gotti (1664-1742), *Theologia Scholastica-Dogmatica juxta Mentem D. Thomae.*

253. Antoninus of Florence (1399-1459), *Summula Confessionalis.*

254. C. Lupus (1612-1681), *Dissertatio de Opinione Probabili.*

255. *Dell'uso moderato dell'opinione probabile* (1765).

256. These two corollaries are printed separately in this text.

First Corollary: A Doubtful Law Does Not Bind

257. Augustine of Hippo (354-430), *Contra Faustum.*

258. Augustine of Hippo (354-430), *De Secundis Nuptiis.*

259. J. L. Berti (1696-1762), *De Theologicis Disciplinis.*

260. Ibid.

261. M. Wigandt (died 1708), *Tribunale Confessariorum et Ordinandorum.*

262. P. Ballerini (1698-1769), *Moralium Actionum Regula seu Quaestio de Opinione Probabili.*

263. Ibid.

264. J. Gonet (1616-1681), *Clypeus Theologiae Thomisticae.*

265. J. V. Patuzzi (1700-1769), *La Causa del Probabilismo Richiamata all'Esame da Alfonso di Liguori e Convinta Novellamente di Falsità.*

266. E. Amort (1692-1775), *Theologia Eclectica Moralis et Scholastica.*

267. Ibid.

268. Ibid.

269. Gregory of Nazianzen (330-389), *Oratio* 59, in *Opera* (Migne Patrologia Latina et Graeca, tom. 35-38).

270. Leo the Great (circa 400-461), *Epistula 90 Sicut quaedam* in *Opera* (Migne, Patrologia Latina et Graeca, tom 54-55).

271. John Chrysostom (347-417), *Opera* (Migne Patrologia Latina et Graeca tom. 47-54).

272. Lactantius, (circa 250-circa 325), *Opera* (Migne, Patrologia Latina et Graeca tom. 6-7).

273. Augustine of Hippo (354-430), *Ad Inquisitionem Januarii.*

274. Ibid.

275. Basil the Great (329-379), *Epistulae* (in Migne Patrologia Latina et Graeca tom. 29-32).

276. Bernard of Clairvaux (1090-1153), *Epistola ad Hugonem de San Vittorio.*

277. Bonaventure of Umbria (circa 1221-1274), *In Quattuor Libros Sententiarum.*

278. Melchior Cano (1509-1560), *Relectiones de Poenitentia.*

279. Ibid.

280. Duns Scotus (circa 1266-1308), *In Quattuor Libros Sententiarum.*

281. Benedict XIV (1675-1758), *Raccolta di Alcuni Notificazioni, Editti ed Istruzioni.*

282. Thomas Aquinas (1225-1274), *Summa Theologiae,* Ia IIae, q. 90, art. 1.

283. Thomas Aquinas (1225-1274), *Summae Theologiae,* Ia IIae, q. 90, art. 4.

284. Thomas Aquinas (1225-1274), *Summae Theologiae,* Ia IIae, q. 90, art. 4 in corpore.

285. Decretum Gratiani, *In Istis* (twelfth century).

286. Thomas Aquinas (1225-1274), *Summa Theologiae,* Ia IIae, q. 90, art. 4, in corpore.

287. Thomas Aquinas (1225-1274), *Summa Theologiae,* Ia IIae, q. 90, art. 4, pr.

288. Thomas Aquinas (1225-1274), *Summa Theologiae,* Ia IIae, q. 90, art. 4, ad 1am.

289. V. Gotti (1664-1742), *Theologia Scholastico - Dogmatica juxta Mentem D. Thomae.*

290. F. Silvius (1581-1649), *Commentarium in Summam S. Thomae et Opuscula.*

291. D. Soto (1494-1560), *De Justitia et Iure.*

292. J. Gerson (1363-1429), *De Vita Spirituali Animae.*

293. J. Gonet (1616-1681), *Clypeus Theologiae Thomisticae.*

294. Thomas Aquinas (1225-1274), *De Veritate,* q. 14, art. 1, in corpore.

295. Gaudé was unable to locate the source of this citation.

296. J. L. Berti (1696-1762), *Opus de Theologicis Disciplinis.*

297. J. V. Patuzzi (1700-1769), *Brevis Instructio de Regula Proxima Humanorum Actionum in Opinionum Delectu.*

298. J. V. Patuzzi (1700-1769), *La Causa del Probabilismo Richiamata all'Esame da Alfonso de Liguori e Convinta Novellamente di Falsità.*

299. Thomas Aquinas (1225-1274), *Summa Theologiae,* Ia IIae, q. 90, art. 4, ad 2am.

300. T. Cajetan (1469-1534), *Commentarium in Summam Theologiam S. Thomae.*

301. P. Collet (1693-1770), *De Legibus.*

302. F. Suarez (1548-1617), *Opere de Legibus.*

303. F. Suarez (1548-1617), *De Censuris.*

304. Aravius (fl. 1640), *Commentarium in Iam IIae, Summae Theologiae.*

305. C. Tapia (died 1664), *Tractatus de Religiosis Rebus.*

306. Castropalaus (1581-1633), *Opera Omnia.*

307. G. Martinez (1575-1637), *Commentarium super Iam IIae D. Thomae.*

308. T. Sanchez (1550-1610), *Opus Morale in Praecepta Decalogi.*

309. H. Villalobos (fl. 1550), *Opiniones in Jure Communes secundum Alfabeti Seriem.*

310. Salmanticenses, confer ch. 1, note 11.

311. Thomas Aquinas (1225-1274), *De Veritate,* q. 17, art. 3.

312. Thomas Aquinas (1225-1274), *Summa Theologiae,* Ia IIae, q. 91, art. 1, ad 2am.

313. A. Duvallius (1564-1638), *Commentarium in Iam IIae.*

314. Ibid.

315. P. de Lorca (1554-1606), *Commentaria et Disputationes in Universam Iam IIae S. Thomae.*

316. Ibid.

317. L. Montesimus (1553-1621), *Commentarium in Iam IIae Divi Thomae.*

318. J. Lorichius (1540-1610), *Thesaurus Novus utriusque Theologiae Theoreticae et Practicae.*

319. Thomas Aquinas (1225-1274), *Summa Theologiae,* Ia IIae, q. 71, art. 6, in corpore.

320. Thomas Aquinas (1225-1274), *Summa Theologiae,* q. 90, art. 4, in corpore.

321. Thomas Aquinas (1225-1274), *Summa Theologiae,* Ia IIae, q. 90, art. 4, in corpore.

322. Thomas Aquinas (1225-1274), *Summa Theologiae,* Ia IIae, q. 91, art. 2.

323. A. Duvallius (1564-1638), *Commentarium in Iam IIae.*

324. F. de Arauxo (1580-1664), *In Iam Iae Partem Divi Thomae.*

325. V. Gotti (1664-1742), *Theologia Scholastico-Dogmatica.*

326. C. Tournely (= P. Collet 1693-1770), *De Legibus.*

327. F. Cuniliati (fl. 1760), *Theologia Moralis.*

328. Thomas Aquinas (1225-1274), *Summa Theologiae,* Ia IIae, q. 90, art. 4, in corpore.

329. V. Gotti (1664-1742), *Theologia Scholastico-Dogmatica.*

330. Ibid.

331. C. Tournely, (= P. Collet 1693-1770), *De Legibus.*

332. F. Silvius (1581-1649), *Commentarii in Summam Sancti Thomae et Opuscula.*

333. Thomas Aquinas (1225-1274), *Summa Theologiae,* Ia IIae, q. 90, art. 4, ad Iam.

334. Thomas Aquinas (1225-1274), *Summa Theologiae,* Ia IIae, q. 91, art. 1, ad IIam.

335. Thomas Aquinas (1225-1274), *Summa Theologiae,* Ia IIae, q. 91, art. 2, in corpore.

336. Antoninus of Florence (1399-1459), *Summa Theologiae.*

337. D. Soto (1494-1560), *De Justitia et Iure.*

338. J. Gerson (1363- 1429), *De Vita Spirituali Animae.*

339. Ibid.

340. F. Silvius (1581-1649), *Commentarii in Summam S. Thomae et Opuscula.*

341. V. Gotti (1664-1742), *Theologia Scholastica-Dogmatica.*

342. F. Silvius (1581-1640), *Commentarii in Summam S. Thomae et Opuscula.*

343. Ibid.

344. Ibid.

345. Ibid.

346. L. Montesimus (1553-1621), *Commentarium in Iam IIae Divi Thomae.*

347. A. Duvallius (1564-1638), *Commentarium in Iam IIae.*

348. P. de Lorca (1554-1606), *Commentaria et disputationes in universam Iam IIae S. Thomae.*

349. F. Cuniliati (died 1759), *Theologia Moralis.*

350. J. Gonet (1616-1681), *Clypeus Theologiae Thomisticae.*

351. Jerome (347-420), *Epistula 121 ad Algasiam.*

352. B. Mastrius (1602-1663), *Theologia Moralis ad mentem DD Seraphici et Subtilis Concinnata.*

353. Gaudé points out that these are not exactly Patuzzi's words.

354. D. Concina (1687-1756), *Theologia Christiana Dogmatico Moralis et Apparatus ad Eamdem.*

355. D. Concina (1687-1756), *Theologia Christiana Contracta in Duos Tomos.*

Second Corollary:
Uncertain Law Cannot Impose Certain Obligation

(The full title of the Second Corollary reads: "A Law that is Uncertain cannot lead to an Obligation that is Certain, because the Freedom of a Person precedes Laws.")

356. Isidore of Seville (circa 560-636), *Opera* (Migne, *Patrologia Graeca et Latina,* tom. 78).

357. Panormitanus (= Nicholas de Tudeschis, 1386-1445), *Commentaria in 5 Libros Decretales et Concilia.*

358. Thomas Aquinas (1225-1274), *Summa Theologiae,* Ia IIae, q. 19, art. 4.

359. Ibid.

360. Thomas Aquinas (1225-1274), *De Veritate,* q. 17, art. 17, corpus.

361. Augustine of Hippo (354-430), *De Libero Arbitrio.*

362. Thomas Aquinas (1225-1274), *De Malo,* q. 3, art. 7, ad 7.

363. Thomas Aquinas (1225-1274), *Summa Theologiae,* Ia IIae, q. 91, art. 1

364. Thomas Aquinas (1225-1274), *Summa Theologiae,* Ia IIae, q. 91, art. 1, pr. 1.

365. Thomas Aquinas (1225-1274), *Summa Theologiae,* Ia IIae, q. 91, art. 1, ad 1am.

366. T. Raymond (1582-1663), *Summa*.

367. Canon *Ponderet, s.d.*

368. Canon *Alligant,* wrongly attributed to John Chrysostom (circa 349-407).

369. Antoninus of Florence (1389-1459), *Summa Theologica*.

370. Gabriel Biel (d. 1495), *Collectoria super 4 Libros Sententiarum*.

371. Thomas Aquinas (1225-1274), *Quaestiones Quodlibetales*, 3, art. 10.

372. J. Nider (circa 1380-1438), *Consolatorium Timoratae Conscientiae*.

373. Thomas Aquinas (1225-1274), *Quaestiones Quodlibetales*, 9, art. 15.

374. Antoninus of Florence (1389-1459), *Summa Theologica*.

375. Thomas Aquinas (1225-1274), *Summa Theologiae,* Ia IIae, q. 19, art. 10.

376. Thomas Aquinas (1225-1274), *Summa Theologiae,* Ia IIae, q. 19, art. 10, pr.

377. Thomas Aquinas (1225-1274), *Summa Theologiae,* Ia IIae, q. 19, art 10, ad Iam.

378. Ibid.

379. J. Gonet (1616-1681), *Clypeus Theologiae Thomisticae*.

380. Attributed to Patuzzi by Alphonsus de Liguori.

381. Thomas Aquinas (1225-1274), *Summa Theologiae,* IIa IIae, q. 104, art. 4.

382. Thomas Aquinas (1225-1274), *Summa Theologiae,* Ia IIae, q. 19, art. 10.

383. Ibid.

384. *Innotescit.*

385. J. Gonet (1616-1681), *Clypeus Theologiae Thomisticae*.

386. J. Gerson (1363-1429), *De Vita Spirituali Animae*.

387 Thomas Aquinas (1225-1274), *Summa Theologiae,* Ia IIae, q. 90, art. 4, ad 1am.

388. Thomas Aquinas (1225-1274), *Summa Theologiae,* Ia IIae, q. 19, art. 4, obj. 3.

389. Thomas Aquinas (1225-1274), *De Veritate,* q. 17, art. 3.

390. Thomas Aquinas (1225-1274), *Summa Theologiae,* Ia IIae, q. 104, art. 4, ad 3am.

391. Antoninus of Florence (1389-1459), *Summa Theologica*.

392. J. V. Patuzzi (1700-1769), *La Causa del Probabilismo*.

393. Antoninus of Florence (1389-1459), *Summa Theologica*.

394. Ibid.

395. J. Nider (died 1438), *Consolatorium Timoratae Conscientiae*.

396. Tabiena (= J. Cagnazzo de Tabia, d. 1521), *Summa Casuum Conscientiae,* sub verbo *scrupulis.*

397. M. Navarrus (1493-1587), *Manuale*.

398. P. Silvester (died 1523), *Summa*.

399. F. Suarez (1548-1617), *De censuris*.

400. J. Angles (died 1587), *Flores Theologicarum Quaestionum in Quartum Librorum Sententiarum.*

401. H. Henriques (1536-1608), *Summa Theologia Moralis.*

402. J. Terillus (1593-1676), *De Conscientia Probabili.*

403. E. Amort (1692-1775), *De Conscientia.*

404. Augustine of Hippo (354-430), *De Fide et Operibus.*

405. Alfonso de Liguori (1696-1787), *Dell'uso moderato dell'opinione probabile* (1765).

406. The edition of Gaudé, which I am using, explains that these are not the words of Aquinas himself.

407. Thomas Aquinas (1225-1274), *Scriptum super Libros Sententiarum,* dist. 31, q. 2., art. 3 ad 3 am.

408. Thomas Aquinas, (1225-1274), *De Veritate,* q. 17, art. 3.

409. J. Cabassutius (1605-1685), *Juiris Canonici Theoria et Praxis.*

410. Bonaventure of Umbria (1221-1274), *Compendium Theologiae Veritatis.*

411. J. Gerson (1363-1429), *De Vita Spirituali Animae.*

412. John Chrysostom (circa 349-407), *Opus Imperfectum in Matthaeum.*

413. F. Suarez (1548-1617), *De Religione.*

414. P. Pallavicinus (1607-1667), *Disputationes, in Iam IIae Divi Thomae.*

415. L. Bancel (1628-1685), *Brevis Universae Theologiae Cursus.*

416. Ibid.

417. Thomas Aquinas (1225-1274), *Summa Theologiae, IIa IIae,* q. 4, art. 8, ad 2am.

418. J. Pontas (1638-1728), *Dictionarium Casuum Conscientiae.*

419. J. Cabassutius (1605-1685), *Iuris Canonici Theoria et Praxis.*

420. Ibid.

421. P. Paludanus (died 1342), *Tertius et Quartus Sententiarum Libri.*

422. F. Victoria (1483-1546), *Summa Sacramentorum Ecclesiae.*

423. F. Adrianus (1459-1523), *Quaestiones de Sacramentis in Quartum Sententiarum.*

424. M. Navarrus (1493-1587), *Manuale.*

425. Ibid.

426. Antoninus of Florence (1389-1459), *Summa Theologica.*

427. Ibid.

428. Ibid.

429. D. Soto (1494-1560), *Commentarium in Quartum Sententiarum.*

430. D. Soto (1494-1560), *De Justitia et Jure.*

Bibliography

Text of Alphonsus de Liguori

Alphonsus de Ligorio. *De Conscientia*, in *Theologia Moralis*, Edited Leonard Gaudé, Rome, Ex Typographia Vaticana, 1905, Tomus Primus, Tractatus Primus, 3–70.

COMMENTARY

When I started on this project more than twenty years ago, my intention was to complete a simple translation of the original text of Alphonsus de Liguori. As I developed the idea of adding a commentary, I needed to fill the substantial gaps in my understanding of the text, its general context, and its implications. I include some of the studies that I found helpful.

Amarante, Alfonso Vincenzo and Marrazzo, Antonio. *Santo, Dottore e Patrono. I Quattri Documenti Pontifici sulla Glorificazione di Sant'Alfonso Maria di Liguori*: Naples, CSsR, 2009.

Amarante, Alfonso V. *La Redazione Alfonsiana del Trattato della Coscienza*: Rome, Gregorian, 1999. [Unpublished STL].

Arboleda, Hermán Valencia and Ferrero, Fabriciano (editors). *Studia et Subsidia de Vita et Operibus S. Alfonsi Mariae de Ligorio (1696–1787)*: Roma, Biblioteca Historica CSsR, 1990.

Berman, Harold J. *Law and Revolution. The Formation of the Western Legal System*: Cambridge, Harvard, 1983.

Capone, Domenico. *La Proposta Morale di Sant'Alfonso. Sviluppo e Attualitá* (a cura di S. B. Botero e S. Majorano): Rome, Edacalf, 1997.

Cunningham, David S. *Faithful Persuasion: In Aid of a Rhetoric of Christian Theology*: Indiana, Notre Dame, 1991.

Ellul, Jacques. *The Theological Foundation of Law*: New York, Seabury, 1969.

Fleming, Julia. *Defending Probablism. The Moral Theology of Juan Caramuel*: Washington, Georgetown, 2006.

Freda, Ambrosio M. *De Institutione e Eruditione Juridica S. Alphonsi M.de Liguori*: Rome, Lateran. 1939. [Unpublished STD].

Gaudé, Leonard. *De Morali Systemate S. Alphonsi M. de Ligorio*: Rome, Cuggiani, 1895.

Gerardi, Renzo. *Storia della Morale*: Bologna, Edizioni Dehoniane, 2003.

Grimali, Luigi and Francesco Saggese (editors). *Il Latino in Tribunale. Brocardi e termini latini in uso nella prassi forense*: Naples, Edizioni Giuridiche, 1999.

Häring, Bernhard. *La Théologie Morale. Idées Maîtresses*: Paris, Cerf, 1992.

Heilig, Michael. *Theologia Moralis S. Alphonsi de Ligorio*. Malignes, Hanicq, 1852.

Hughes, Gerard J. *Moral Decisions*: London, Darton, Longman & Todd, 1980.

Hurtubise, Pierre. *La Casuistique dans tous ses États*: Ottawa, Novalis, 2005.

Johnstone, Brian V. "Erroneous Conscience in *Veritatis Splendor* and the Theological Tradition." In *The Splendor of Accuracy: An Examination of the Assertions made by Veritatis Splendor*, ed. Joseph A. Selling and Jan Jans, 114–135. Kampen–The Netherlands: Kos-Pharos 1994.

Jones, Frederick M. *Alphonsus de Liguori: Saint of Bourbon Naples 1696-1787*: Dublin, Gill and Macmillan, 1992.

Keenan, James F. *A History of Moral Theology in the Twentieth Century*: New York, Continuum, 2010.

Kittsteiner, Heinz. *La Naissance de la Conscience Morale au Seuil de l'Âge Moderne*: Paris, Cerf, 1997.

MacIntyre, Alisdair. *A Short History of Ethics*: London and New York, Routledge, 1998.

Mahoney, John, *The Making of Moral Theology*: Oxford, Clarendon, 1987.

Majorano, Sabatino. *La Coscienza*: Milan, San Paolo, 1994.

McCormick, Richard A. *Ambiguity in Moral Choice*: Marquette Theology Lectures, 1973.

Nussbaum, Martha. *The Fragility of Goodness*: New York, Cambridge, 1986.

Orlandi, Giuseppe. *Alfonso de Liguori Scrittore*: Salerno, Segno, 1998.

Perrini. Matteo. *Filosofia e Conscienza*: Brescia, Morcelliana, 2008.

Ratzinger, Joseph Cardinal. *On Conscience*: San Francisco, Ignatius, 2007.

Rey-Mermet, Théodule. *Moral Choices. The Moral Theology of Saint Alphonsus Liguori* (translated by Paul Laverdure): Liguori, 1998.

Shanley, Brian J. *The Thomist Tradition*: Dordrecht/Boston/London, Kluwer, 2002.

Strohm, Paul. *Conscience. A very short Introduction*: Oxford, University Press, 2011.

Testa, Lorenzo. *La Questione della Coscienza Erronea*: Milan, Glossa, 2006.

Tutino, Stefania. *Uncertainty in Post-Reformation Catholicism*: Oxford, University Press, 2018.

Vereecke, Louis. *De Guillaume d'Ockham à Saint Alphonse de Liguori*: Rome, Biblioteca Historica CSsR, 1986.

Vidal, Marciano. *La Morale di Sant'Alfonso dal Rigorismo alla Benignitá*: Rome, Edacalf, 2006.

ABOUT FR. RAPHAEL GALLAGHER

Fr. Raphael Gallagher, CSsR, taught moral theology
for nearly four decades and has studied this text on
the subject by St. Alphonsus Liguori for more than
twenty years. Born in Ireland and ordained in 1969, Fr.
Gallagher earned a BA from University College Galway
(now named National University of Ireland Galway),
with a licentiate (STL) and doctorate (SThD) from the
Alphonsian Academy of Rome's Pontifical Lateran
University. He taught moral theology in Ireland, the
United States, and Italy. He has published widely on
moral and pastoral issues. During the time that he was
an invited professor at the Alphonsian Academy (1994-
2014), Fr. Gallagher was the editor of the journal *Studia
Moralia* for six years.

www.ingramcontent.com/pod-product-compliance
Lightning Source LLC
Chambersburg PA
CBHW020844270326
41928CB00006B/540